Emerging Services Sector and Inclusiveness

Emerging Services Sector and Inclusiveness:

Evidence from India

Edited by

Pralok Gupta

Cambridge Scholars Publishing

Emerging Services Sector and Inclusiveness: Evidence from India

Edited by Pralok Gupta

This book first published 2015

Cambridge Scholars Publishing

Lady Stephenson Library, Newcastle upon Tyne, NE6 2PA, UK

British Library Cataloguing in Publication Data
A catalogue record for this book is available from the British Library

ISBN (10): 1-4438-7614-3
ISBN (13): 978-1-4438-7614-8

Dedicated to my parents

The Late Smt. Krishna Devi

and

The Late Sh. Surya Prakash Gupta

TABLE OF CONTENTS

LIST OF TABLES

LIST OF FIGURES

ACKNOWLEDGMENTS

At the outset, I would like to thank Prof. Abhijit Das, Head of the Centre for WTO Studies, IIFT, New Delhi, for his guidance and constant support during the writing of this manuscript. I would also like to express my gratitude towards all faculty members and staff of the Centre for WTO Studies for their invaluable help. Last but not least, I thank my family, Vaishali (my wife) and Arshabh (my son), for their support and for bearing with me while I devoted my time to working on this manuscript at home.

Pralok Gupta

PREFACE

The services sector consists of a wide range of activities including transportation, communication, financial, business and professional services, community, social and personal services and government services. Many services act as important inputs to the production of other goods and services. As an economy progresses, the contribution of the services sector becomes more and more important. The world over, the services sector has emerged as one of the largest and fastest-growing sectors and made significant contributions to global output. The Indian story is no different and this sector has emerged as the most dynamic and important sector in the post-liberalization era. It has increased its contribution to the Indian economy not only in terms of GDP, but also in exports. However, one area where the services sector has not yet contributed significantly is employment creation. Thus, critics have raised questions on the inclusivity of India's services sector-led growth story.

Against this backdrop, this book is a compilation of selected papers devoted to understanding and analyzing the role of the services sector in GDP, trade and inclusive growth in the Indian economy. Most of these papers were presented during the National Conference on "Trade in Services in India and Inclusive Growth Paradigm: Emerging Opportunities and Future Challenges", held on August 22nd-23rd, 2013, in New Delhi, organized by the Centre for WTO Studies, Indian Institute of Foreign Trade, New Delhi. The conference was aimed at discussing research on the emerging role of services in India's foreign trade and the opportunities and challenges created by the services sector boom in the Indian economy. The papers presented during the conference examined specific issues related to the growth of and trade in the services sector in India, such as outsourcing, foreign direct investment, migration, employment, etc., and also analyzed sector specific issues in various services.

The first three chapters of this book are devoted to understanding the role of the services sector in the Indian economy within the broad parameters of growth, employment, balance of payment, trade cycles etc. These are followed by a chapter on linking the services trade with migration, which has attracted the attention of policy makers recently. The next three chapters discuss FDI in the services sector, with sector specific case studies dealing with retail and aviation. The last two chapters are devoted to sectoral case studies of two important service sectors in India, namely IT-BPO services and insurance services.

The first chapter of the book discusses the unemployment aspect of India's liberalization of the services sector and the related adjustment policies that India has adopted to minimize the adverse effects of such liberalization on the employment scenario in India. It highlights how the employment scenario has changed over the years in India without any significant increase in the share of the services sector in job creation, despite its significant contribution to India's GDP. It explains the possible reasons for the paradox and discusses the mitigating measures adopted by India to counter this situation.

Chapter Two analyzes the relationship between the services trade, economic growth and external stabilization based on the Indian experience. It states that the quantum, quality and financing of the current account deficit (CAD) have recently emerged as a major concern for Indian policy makers, faced with a gloomy macro-economic scenario of decelerating growth, large-scale capital exit from stock markets and massive rupee depreciation. This paper finds that private transfers have been more crisis-prone as compared to net services exports in the case of the Indian economy. It suggests that adopting policies that promote India's services exports, diversify its export markets, and raise its export competitiveness globally is a much better recipe for India's external stabilization.

Chapter Three empirically analyzes the growth and cycles of India's trade in services for the period 1950-2010. Using Lee and Strazicich's structural break test, the study tests whether the growth in services trade has evolved gradually over a period of time or whether it was a response to policy changes. The structural break test does not reveal a significant break in services exports and imports. Hence, the study finds that the growth in services trade evolved gradually over the years. Further, the study also addresses the question of whether the integration of the sector with the rest of the world has paved the way for the transmission of external cyclical upturns and downturns to India. The study identifies three cycles during the period 1950-2010; the first one from 1963-64 to 1981-82; the second from 1981-82 to 1999-2000 and the third with a short peak in the post-2000 period. Moreover, it finds that services exports propel cycles, as the shocks in exports exhibit a higher intensity than those in imports.

Chapter Four attempts to explore the growing links between trade and migration by looking at the trade in services and linking it with the migration question. It analyzes the only multilateral agreement governing the temporary movement of workers – the World Trade Organization's General Agreement on Trade in Services. It also analyzes regional trade agreements; however, it confines itself to only those regional trade agreements that have been entered into by a regional organization.

In Chapter Five, an attempt has been made to evaluate the performance of the services sector in the pre- and post-global crisis period in terms of FDI and its corresponding contribution to the economy. For empirical analysis, the variables selected are GDP, FDI and Gross Capital Formation Rate (GCFR) during 1991-2012. The analysis is done on the basis of the panel unit root test, panel regression analysis, the Granger causality test and the co-integration test. The services sector is segregated into financial and non-financial services, construction, trade, hotel, transportation and telecommunication, insurance, real estate, and community, social and personal services for better understanding of the sector at the micro level. An attempt has also been made to assess the expected impact of global recession on the Indian economy at large and the services sector in particular. This paper argues that an economy that is growing only on the basis of services sector growth is like building a castle in the air without strong foundations.

Chapter Six gives an understanding of the conditions laid down in the 2013 FDI Policy for FDI in the aviation sector in India. It analyzes the impact of the 2013 policy on, and highlights the determinants of, FDI in the airline industry. The objective is to analyze the challenges in the path of FDI in the airline industry, identify gaps and analyze them, and draw up an action plan. The paper argues that there is urgent need for more reforms in the Indian aviation sector to maximize FDI inflows and the consequent benefits to passengers, the ailing airline industry, and the economy at large.

Chapter Seven examines the case of FDI in retail in India, which has been a very hotly debated issue in recent times. The retail industry in India is still at a nascent and developing stage in the economy. It has attracted attention from foreign investors, but the adverse effects of FDI in retail have been neglected by the government. Foreign direct investment (FDI) in retail – given the current economic realities of India and the lack of equitable distribution of the Gross National Product (GNP) – might do more harm than good. The paper argues that although large format retailing and the entry of FDI will bring many good things with it, policy makers must also be cognizant of the harm it may do. The paper further argues that while large format retailing is inevitable, we must not hasten it. Rather, the task right now should be to change the composition of GNP and create jobs so that the rush into self-employed retailing slows down.

Chapter Eight presents the case study of an important service sector in India – the IT-BPO sector. India is at the forefront of the rapidly evolving global IT Business Process Outsourcing (BPO), now known as Business

Process Management, market and is well established as a 'destination of choice'. Today, the superlatives such as 'Soft Superpower', 'IT Hub' and 'World's IT Capital' have become synonymous with India. This research paper examines the transformation of the IT/ITeS sector since 1991 in general and since 2008, after the sub-prime crisis in the USA, in particular. The focus of the paper is to re-examine the composition, size and direction of business outsourcing over the past two and a half decades. The paper recommends that to strengthen its global competitiveness, India should increasingly diversify its IT/ITeS business to move higher in the value chain, explore business opportunities in Asian and African countries to reduce over-dependence on the West, and build up its infrastructure for a wider spread across the nation.

Chapter Nine presents a case study of the insurance sector in India. The insurance sector, as a branch of financial services, occupies an important place in the economy, since risk, which can be hedged, has increased enormously in every sphere. The life insurance market has played an increasingly substantial role within the insurance industry. The paper endeavors to show the relationship between the level of insurance penetration and Gross Domestic Product (GDP) in India. In addition, a state-wise analysis of insurance penetration and per capita net state domestic product has also been taken into consideration. The chapter observes that lack of financial awareness causes lower savings in financial instruments, which has contributed to the low level of insurance penetration. It argues that in order to capitalize on growth in the economy and improve penetration, the insurance industry will need to tap not only public investment but also private and foreign investment.

CHAPTER ONE

SERVICES SECTOR LIBERALIZATION, UNEMPLOYMENT AND TRADE-RELATED ADJUSTMENT POLICIES IN INDIA[1]

PRALOK GUPTA

Introduction

The rapid growth of India's services sector in the post-reform era (1991 onwards) has contributed to the country's recent emergence as one of the fastest-growing economies in the world. India's services sector not only remained resilient during and after the global financial crisis but also provided significant support to overall GDP growth. As a result, India was ranked 10th and 12th in the world in terms of overall gross domestic product (GDP) and services GDP respectively in 2012. The compound annual growth rate (CAGR) of services for the period 2001-14 in India was 8.5 per cent, second in the world only to China. Given its growth performance, the contribution of the services sector (including construction) to overall GDP has increased sharply, from 41 per cent in 1990-91 to 64.8 per cent in 2013-14 (Government of India 2014, 175). The CAGR of services sector GDP for the period 2000-01 to 2013-14 was higher than the CAGR of overall GDP. The emerging services sector in India consists of sophisticated and technology-driven services like IT and telecommunications, infrastructural services like ports and railways, business services like consultancy and professional services, traditional services like barbers and plumbers and many other varieties of service.

---

[1] This chapter is based on Gupta, P. (2013a) "Paradox of High Growth and Low Employment", Yojana, Govt. of India, Vol. 57 (October); pp 41-44 and Gupta P. (2013b), 'Chapter on Services Sector in India' in the Mid-Year Review of Indian Economy by National Council for Applied Economic Research, New Delhi.

The services sector has also facilitated India's integration with the world economy through trade and investment. Services exports have grown significantly, from less than USD 7 billion in 1995 to over USD 141 billion by 2012. India's share in global services exports has risen from 0.5 per cent in 1995 to over 3 per cent in 2012. The sector's share in the country's exports rose from around 18 per cent in 1995 to over 39 per cent in 2011 (UNCTAD 2013).

The current dynamism of India's services sector is largely a reflection of domestic liberalization and growing links with external markets. However, there has been debate in India over the implications of liberalization on the services sector and of services-led growth on employment creation. It is interesting to note that, whereas some services like tourism services are labor intensive and have high employment elasticity, some others, such as IT and telecom, are less labor intensive and have low employment elasticity. As a consequence, in spite of a significant jump in services' share in GDP, services' contribution to employment increased only marginally over the liberalization period in India. Due to this phenomenon, many economists have criticized India's growth story as "jobless growth", i.e. there is high growth in the Indian economy but jobs are not being created. This has compelled the government to start focusing on policies and programmes that not only mitigate the adverse effects of such liberalization but also help in creating additional employment opportunities.

Against this backdrop, this paper focuses on the unemployment aspect of India's services liberalization. It discusses the adjustment policies that India has adopted to minimize the adverse effects of this liberalization on the employment scenario in India and to increase services sector employment.

Services Liberalization and Employment in India

Services liberalization has been actively pursued in India by adopting relaxed and liberal regulatory policies from time to time. Apart from fulfilling the obligations resulting from multilateral commitments and offers made in its regional trade agreements (RTAs), India has undertaken significant liberalization in many services unilaterally. As a result, the level of autonomous services liberalization (unilateral liberalization) is much higher than the committed level in either the WTO or the RTAs. The equity limit for foreign direct investment (FDI) has been progressively increased in various services and, in many services, 100 per cent FDI is allowed, either through the automatic approval route or the prior approval route.

The liberalization of India's services sector and a continuous rise in its share in India's GDP over the years have not resulted in corresponding employment generation in this sector. Table 1.1 shows the share of employment per sector in India for the years 1993-94, 2004-05, 2007-08 and 2009-10. The data reveals that, while the share of employment in the tertiary sector (predominantly services) has increased over the years, the primary sector (predominantly agriculture) is still the dominant employer. The share of the primary sector in employment fell sharply between 1993-94 and 2004-05. The consequent rise in the share of employment in the secondary (predominantly industry) and tertiary sectors was fairly balanced between the two.

Table 1.1: Share of Employment per Sector in India (%), 1993-94, 2004-05, 2007-08 and 2009-10[2]

Year	Primary	Secondary	Tertiary
1993–94	64.5	14.3	21.2
2004–05	57.0	18.2	24.8
2007–08	55.9	18.7	25.4
2009-10	53.2	21.5	25.3

Source: Government of India, Ministry of Finance, Economic Survey, 2010–11 and 2012-13

This observed trend for India is in contrast to the trend in developed and some developing countries, in which not only has the contribution of the services sector to employment increased over time with the process of development, but services have also become the dominant player in employing human resources in these economies. For instance, by the beginning of 2000, in several OECD countries, about three quarters of employees were working in services (D'Agostino, Serafini and Ward-Warmedinger 2006, 7). Many Asian countries, such as Korea, also have a significantly higher share of services in their overall employment. Barring China and India, all the top 15 countries (in terms of services GDP) have high shares of both services GDP and services employment. Although neither India nor China has a high share of services employment, they are

[2] The sectoral contribution of services does not include the construction sector. If we include construction within services, the employment contribution of services becomes around 36 per cent in 2009-10.

different from each other. Whereas China has low shares of both services income and employment, in India, on the other hand, the services sector has a high share in income but a lower share in employment. The gap between the shares of services income and employment in India is also widening, from 27.3 percentage points in 2001 to 28.8 percentage points in 2012 (Government of India 2014, 174).

If we analyze employment data at the state level, it is observed that there are widespread differences in employment in various sectors across India. While some states, such as Kerala, have a high share of employment in the services sector, states like Chhattisgarh, Madhya Pradesh and Gujarat have relatively low shares of people employed in services. Some north-eastern states like Sikkim, Tripura, and Manipur have a high share of employment in the services sector. Construction, trade, hotels, and restaurants and public administration, education, and community services are the three major employment-providing services in different states (Government of India 2012, 231).

There are also big differences between the shares of the services sector in employment in rural and urban India. The share is very high in urban areas in most states compared to rural areas. This implies that services liberalization and services-led growth have been limited more or less to urban India and the fruits of such liberalization and growth have not percolated to rural India. A natural corollary to this imbalance is that, of late, there has been a lot of internal migration in India from rural to urban areas due to the absence or lack of employment opportunities in rural areas. This migration has increased the challenges faced by urban civic bodies, which already find it difficult to meet the growing demands posed by rapid urbanization in India. Table 1.2 shows sector-wise rural and urban employment per 1,000 employed people for various Indian states.

Table 1.2: State-wise Employment in Different Sectors in Rural and Urban India in 2009-10 (per 1000 employed people)

State/UT	Agriculture and Allied		Industry		Services with Construction		Services without Construction	
	Rural	Urban	Rural	Urban	Rural	Urban	Rural	Urban
Andhra Pradesh	687	53	97	241	217	705	150	583
Arunachal Pradesh	757	140	32	41	213	817	158	722
Assam	725	27	38	137	257	833	222	757
Bihar	669	146	53	121	279	732	174	609
Chhattisgarh	849	53	39	282	112	666	83	553
Delhi	0	1	120	285	879	712	542	682
Goa	239	14	365	289	397	696	353	552
Gujarat	783	53	62	306	156	641	112	576
Haryana	598	53	98	319	304	627	195	511
Himachal Pradesh	629	85	53	149	320	767	167	676
Jammu & Kashmir	597	110	84	227	316	662	218	552
Jharkhand	548	52	92	160	361	787	145	602
Karnataka	757	94	67	221	176	686	132	558
Kerala	357	110	132	178	511	711	357	570
Madhya Pradesh	824	98	48	203	128	700	62	569
Maharashtra	794	47	52	236	154	716	116	638
Manipur	534	205	90	118	377	677	240	604
Meghalaya	707	58	56	65	236	877	178	780
Mizoram	806	360	14	53	180	587	128	499
Nagaland	741	219	17	35	241	745	200	684
Odisha	676	103	84	215	240	683	144	549

Punjab	618	83	81	249	298	669	168	552
Rajasthan	633	70	54	186	312	743	110	595
Sikkim	539	0	48	99	414	901	282	874
Tamil Nadu	637	136	117	276	246	586	146	482
Tripura	306	21	63	89	633	891	244	716
Uttarakhand	695	54	41	199	263	747	131	629
Uttar Pradesh	669	91	76	257	257	653	134	551
West Bengal	563	36	173	279	265	683	206	621
A & N Islands	430	30	91	98	477	873	330	766
Chandigarh	31	22	145	122	826	856	629	778
Dadra & Nagar Haveli	591	38	160	632	251	332	155	315
Daman & Diu	548	394	340	177	110	430	106	398
Lakshadweep	452	277	57	164	491	558	361	483
Pondicherry	461	29	144	201	396	770	238	647
All India	**679**	**75**	**80**	**242**	**241**	**683**	**147**	**582**

Source: Government of India, Ministry of Finance, Economic Survey, 2011-12

Trade-Related Adjustment Policies

Trade-related adjustment policies are common in many developed countries. For instance, the USA established the Trade Adjustment Assistant (TAA) Program in 1974, which aimed to assist workers and enterprises negatively affected by trade reforms or changes in trade flows. The TAA Program is a federally funded programme, with no cost to employers. It aims to help workers adversely affected by foreign imports or job shifts to a foreign country. It provides assistance to eligible workers in the form of re-employment services, training, job searches, relocation, and support benefits in the form of Trade Readjustment Allowances (TRA) and/or Alternative/Re-employment Trade Adjustment Assistance (ATAA/RTAA) for older workers (United States Department of Labor 2012).

Similarly, the EU introduced the European Globalization Adjustment Fund in 2006 (Francois, Jansen and Peters 2011, 213). The fund provides support to people who lose their jobs as a result of major structural changes in world trade patterns due to globalization. For instance, the fund provides appropriate support when workers are laid off because a large company shuts down or production is moved outside the EU or as a result of a global financial or economic crisis. The fund has a maximum annual budget of EUR 150 million for the period 2014-2020 and can fund up to 60 per cent of the cost of projects designed to help workers made redundant find others job or set up their own businesses (European Commission 2014).

However, such adjustment programmes and policies are not very common in developing countries. As far as trade-related adjustment policies in India with specific reference to services liberalization and unemployment are concerned, the policies and programmes of the government are not specifically designed to cater to trade-related adjustments. Rather, they are designed to solve the underlying problem of unemployment and related issues, which have been intensified because of the liberalization of the economy in general and the services sector in particular. Thus, such policies *de facto* become trade-related adjustment policies in a broader sense. The definition of trade-related adjustment policies needs to consider both *de jure* and *de facto* cases of such adjustment policies and programmes, i.e. it should consider not only those policies that are specifically designed for trade-related adjustments (*de jure* cases) but also those that are not primarily formulated for such adjustments but assist in adjusting the adverse effects that either occur purely as a consequence of trade liberalization or are intensified by this liberalization (*de facto* cases). It also needs to be understood that trade-related adjustment policies need not be corrective in nature. Rather, they may include proactive policies and programs that the government initiates in order to overcome the likely negative effects of liberalization.

In this context, it is worth mentioning a few policies and programs of the Government of India that were intended to solve the employment generation problem in the services sector during the liberalization period. First, in order to tackle the "jobless" growth phenomenon associated with services sector liberalization, the Government of India has started focusing on services that are more labor intensive, such as tourism, retail distribution, construction, health services etc. The government, both at the federal and state level, has initiated various programs for capacity building in these service sectors. For example, in the tourism sector, the State Government of Gujarat has set up a Centre for Tourism and Hospitality Management as a public private partnership (PPP) initiative to train service providers, guides and tourism personnel, targeting specifically the weaker sections of society. The Ministry of Tourism of the Government of India implemented various schemes, such as Product Infrastructure Development for Destination and Circuits (PIDDC), Overseas Promotion and Publicity including market development assistance, assistance for academic institutions for capacity building for service providers, assistance with large revenue generating projects, etc. during the period of 2007-12. The Approach Paper to the 12th Five-year Plan of the Government of India recommended a "pro-poor tourism" approach to increase the net benefits to the poor from tourism and to ensure that tourism growth contributes to employment and poverty reduction (Government of India 2011).

An important step taken by the government to mitigate the adverse effects of liberalization is to set up specialized funds for workers in the unorganized sector, as they are the most vulnerable section of society and are prone to being side-lined in the process of development. The Ministry of Labour has set up welfare funds for various categories and sub-categories of workers in the unorganized sector, including the services sector. For instance, the government has enacted central legislation for builders and other construction workers to create welfare funds at the state level. There are around 20 million construction workers in the country. A small levy is collected on the basis of the cost of a construction project, which makes up the corpus of the welfare fund for construction workers. The welfare fund model has successfully been implemented by various states for various categories of workers. For example, the state of Tamil

Nadu runs 11 welfare boards for workers including construction workers, truck drivers, footwear workers, handloom and silk weaving workers.[3]

Another relevant issue related to the unorganized sector in India is that so far, most of the education and skill development has been geared toward the needs of the organized sector, and the unorganized sector has remained untouched. This has resulted in unfavorable and sometimes extremely miserable conditions for people working in the unorganized sector, which includes primarily labor intensive services such as construction work, midwifery, domestic work, barbering, vegetable and fruit vending, newspaper vending etc. However, the government has started focusing on employment-related issues in the unorganized sector, including social security measures. According to the National Sample Survey Organization (NSSO) survey conducted in 2004-05, there were 433 million workers in the unorganized sector, constituting about 94 per cent of the total labor force in India. Recognizing the need to provide social security to unorganized workers, the government enacted the Unorganized Workers' Social Security Act in 2008.

The Act provides for the constitution of a Nation Social Security Board to recommend social security schemes viz. life and disability cover, maternity health benefits, old age protection and any other benefit as may be determined by the government for unorganized workers. The government also launched the "Rashtriya Swasthya Bima Yojana" (National Health Insurance Policy) for "Below Poverty Line" (BPL) families in the unorganized sector in 2007. The scheme, providing for smartcard-based cashless health insurance cover of INR 30,000 per family per annum on a family floater basis, has been in operation since 2008. The scheme has been effective in terms of its coverage, as more than 25 million families have been covered under the scheme as of October 31st, 2011.[4] It is to be noted that although these schemes are generic in nature and not specifically focused on trade reforms in services, they also work as trade adjustment policies (*de facto* cases) as unorganized workers, many of whom are in the services sector, are the ones most affected by the adverse consequences of trade, particularly during the initial years of liberalization.

The government has also imparted skill upgrade training to those who may get adversely affected by services sector reforms, including

---

[3] Unorganized Sector in India: Social Security and Welfare Funds, http://labour.nic.in/ss/UNORGANISEDSECTORININDIA-SocialSecurityandWelfareFunds.pdf

[4] Social Security Schemes for Workers in Unorganized Sector, http://equalityindia.wordpress.com/2011/11/23/social-security-schemes-for-workers-in-unorganized-sector/

increasing computerization, in India. The Director General of Employment and Training, Ministry of Labour, initiated the Skill Development Initiative Scheme (SDIS) based on Modular Employable Skills (MES) in May 2007. An important feature of this scheme is that it focuses on providing short-term courses to poor and less educated people, as they cannot afford long-term training programmes due to higher entry qualification requirements, opportunity costs, etc. (DGE&T 2014). The government also formulated the "National Policy on Skill Development" in 2009. The policy is a guiding document for the implementation of various skill development programs in the country. The policy has set a target of skilling 500 million people by the year 2022 (Sharma 2010, 5).

The government has also proactively included conditions that will assist in generating employment in India while further liberalizing its services sector. For instance, in retail distribution services, the government has increased the foreign equity limit from 51 per cent to 100 per cent in single brand retail and up to 51 per cent in multi-brand retail. In order to ensure employment generation in this sector, the government has imposed conditions such as mandatory sourcing of at least 30 per cent of the value of products sold from small and medium industries/village and cottage industries, artisans and craftsmen for proposals involving FDI in multi-brand retail and over 51 per cent in single brand retail (DIPP 2014).

Thus, the Government of India has taken steps, both reactively and proactively, to solve the unemployment problem, which arose out of the structural deficiencies of the economy but has been intensified by the liberalization of the economy over the past two decades. As services are becoming more and more important in the Indian economy, policies are being adjusted to create enough employment opportunities in the services sector so that the liberalization and reforms in India's services sector can also be associated with high employment generation.

Conclusion

There has been no significant increase in the service sector's share in employment considering the very large increase in its share in GDP during the last two decades. Broader based growth within the sector is required to ensure balanced, equitable and employment-oriented growth that is linked to the rest of the economy. Although the government has started focusing on the issues of "jobless growth" related to services liberalization, no government policies or programs have been designed specifically to tackle this problem. More government intervention and targeted adjustment policies are required to generate employment in India's services sector.

Further reforms in infrastructure, the regulatory environment and FDI liberalization will also be required to diversify the sources of growth and hence increase employment opportunities and provide the required momentum for further growth.

References

Antonello D'Agostino, Roberta Serafini and Melanie Ward-Warmedinger. 2006. *Sectoral Explanations of Employment in Europe – The Role of Services*. Frankfurt: European Central Bank Working Paper Series No. 625.

Directorate General of Employment and Training (DGE&T). 2014. "Skill Development Initiative Scheme (SDIS)." Accessed December 12. http://dget.nic.in/content/innerpage/introduction-sdis.php.

Department of Industrial Policy and Promotion (DIPP). 2014. "Consolidated FDI Policy, April 2014." Accessed December 10.

http://dipp.gov.in/English/Policies/FDI_Circular_2014.pdf.

European Commission. 2014. "European Globalisation Adjustment Fund." Accessed December 01.

http://ec.europa.eu/social/main.jsp?catId=326.

Francois Joseph, Marion Jansen and Ralf Peters. 2011. "Trade, Adjustment Costs and Assistance: The Labour Market Dynamics." In *Trade and Employment: From Myths to Facts*, edited by Marion Jansen, Ralf Peters and Jose Manuel Salazar-Xirinachs, 213-252. Geneva: International Labour Office.

Government of India. 2014. *Economic Survey 2013–14*. New Delhi: Ministry of Finance.

—. 2012. *Economic Survey 2011–12*. New Delhi: Ministry of Finance.

—. 2011a. *Economic Survey 2010–11*. New Delhi: Ministry of Finance.

—. 2011a. *Report of the Working Group on Tourism for XII Five Year Plan*. New Delhi: Planning Commission of India.

Gupta, Pralok. 2013a. "Paradox of High Growth and Low Employment." In *Yojana*, Govt. of India, Vol. 57 (October), 41-44.

—. 2013b. "Services Sector in India." In *Mid-Year Review of Indian Economy*, New Delhi: National Council for Applied Economic Research.

Sharma, Yash Pal. 2010. "Skill Development Programmes in India." Background Note on South-South Study Visit to China and India on Skills and Technical and Vocational Education and Training. November 1-12.

'Social Security Schemes for Workers in Unorganized Sector.' Accessed July 11, 2013. http://equalityindia.wordpress.com/2011/11/23/social-security-schemes-for-workers-in-unorganized-sector/

UNCTAD. 2013. 'UNCTADStat: UNCTAD Database on International Trade in services.' Access November 10. http://unctadstat.unctad.org.

United States Department of Labor. 2012. "What is Trade Adjustment Assistance?" Last modified June 22. http://www.doleta.gov/tradeact/factsheet.cfm.

'Unorganised Sector in India: Social Security and Welfare Funds.' Accessed July 11, 2013.

http://labour.nic.in/ss/UNORGANISEDSECTORININDIA-SocialSecurityandWelfareFunds.pdf

CHAPTER TWO

THE RELATIONSHIP BETWEEN THE SERVICES TRADE, ECONOMIC GROWTH AND EXTERNAL STABILISATION: EVIDENCE FROM INDIA[1]

MINI P. THOMAS

Introduction

International trade in services started expanding rapidly in the last decades of the twentieth century, growing much faster than both world output and world merchandise trade. Global trade in services increased from USD 1798.9 billion in 1991 to USD 8699.8 billion by 2012 (UNCTAD 2013). International trade in services gained importance in policy circles after the General Agreement on Trade in Services (GATS) came into being in 1995. Developing countries now account for a quarter of the world trade in services. In spite of a rising contribution to services trade by developing countries, developed countries accounted for 67 per cent of world services exports and 59 per cent of world services imports in 2012 (UNCTAD 2013). Services trade brings along technology, which is a source of endogenous growth. New economy services, i.e. services that are increasingly tradable internationally on account of advances in Information and Communication Technology and raise productivity growth, have emerged as a powerful force contributing to the economic growth and external stabilisation of many countries in recent years.

The emergence of service sector-led growth in India is in consensus with the growing importance of services trade globally. The economic

[1] This paper is a part of the author's ongoing doctoral dissertation. The author is very grateful to her PhD supervisor Prof. M. R. Narayana for his invaluable suggestions and comments at various stages of development of this paper. However, the usual disclaimers apply.

reforms initiated in India after the emergence of the balance of payments (BoP) crisis in 1990-91 resulted in the Government of India reversing its policy of import substitution, followed since independence. A policy of export-oriented growth was adopted, following the footsteps of East Asian countries. India's international trade in services benefited immensely from this change in policy stance, and received a further boost when India became a signatory to the WTO in 1995. As per GOI (2012), the share of services in India's total GDP rose from 43 per cent in 1990-91 to 59 per cent in 2011-12. The service sector's annual GDP growth rate has been higher than the country's overall GDP since 1997-98. Services exports have been growing even faster than services GDP in the post-reform period, reflecting the export-oriented nature of India's service sector growth. India exhibits a strong advantage in services compared to goods. India's share in global services exports stood at 3.2 per cent in 2011, whereas its share in global merchandise exports was only 1.66 per cent for the same year (WTO 2012).

Services exports also have the potential to bring about the external stabilisation of the Indian economy. Since the advent of the global economic recession in 2008-09, India's external sector has been under growing pressure, as is evident from the widening current account deficit (CAD). The CAD in 2011-12 was 4.2 per cent of GDP, historically the highest ever (even higher than the CAD of 3 per cent of GDP during the peak of the 1991 BoP crisis). The current account balance, which averaged nil over the Tenth Plan period, deteriorated during the Eleventh Plan to an average CAD of 2.4 per cent. The Approach Paper to the Twelfth Five-year Plan (GOI 2011, 21) stated that for prudent management of the external account, it is desirable to restrict the CAD to an average below 2.5 per cent of India's GDP over the plan period. This is the CAD that would be commensurate with the 12th Plan growth target of 9-9.5 per cent. Excessive CAD tends to make an economy vulnerable to external debt and currency crisis, and brings in its wake financial instability, substantial output and welfare losses. An RBI study (R. Goyal 2012, 1) has concluded that a CAD of between 2.4 and 2.8 per cent of GDP is sustainable over the medium term, on the assumptions that GDP growth ranges between 6-8 per cent, inflation hovers around the 5 per cent level, and the interest rate and size of capital flows broadly follow their recent trends.

There are three different perspectives on current account balance: a domestic perspective based on national income and product accounts; an international perspective based on trade flows in goods and services, and another international perspective based on the flows and holdings of financial assets. Each perspective involves a decision to focus on certain variables or economic relationships and to de-emphasise or ignore other variables and relationships (Mann 2002, 134). This study will focus on the second perspective, based on international trade flows in goods and services. It has also been noted that the CAD in the Indian economy is influenced more by external factors, such as oil supply shocks or the sudden collapse of export markets, than domestic saving and investment rates (A. Goyal 2012). Given this background, this paper attempts to explore the relationship between services trade, economic growth and external stabilisation in the Indian economy. External stabilisation is defined as "current account stabilisation" for the purposes of this study. India's international trade in services is measured in terms of "net exports of non-factor services". India's economic growth is measured in terms of gross domestic product at market prices (base year 2004-05). The Reserve Bank of India's (RBI) definition of the service sector, inclusive of "construction activities", has been adopted for this study.

Review of Literature

Services have not figured prominently in economic growth theory, and have only recently been highlighted in international trade theory. However, the relationship between international trade and economic growth has been extensively studied in literature. Proponents of the export-led growth hypothesis (Beckerman 1965; Balassa 1978; Feder 1982) have argued that export growth leads to an expansion in production via the foreign trade multiplier, economies of scale and technological innovation. A few others (Vernon 1966; Krugman 1984; Bhagwati 1988) have focused on the reverse causality channel, wherein increases in skilled labour and technology in the domestic economy stimulate productivity gains, which give rise to comparative advantages in certain sectors, and eventually export expansion. Endogenous growth models emphasise imports as an important channel for long-run economic growth, providing domestic firms with access to foreign technology and R and D knowledge (Grossman and Helpman 1991; Lee 1995). Oulton (2001) proved that international trade in services increases overall growth, because greater outsourcing of services by productive firms in non-stagnant sectors entails a reallocation of factors, which increases overall output and aggregate productivity.

Pradhan (2010) examined the export-led growth hypothesis for the Indian economy. The time frame of his study was from 1970-71 to 2009-10, and covered exports of both goods and services. Using the Engle-Granger approach to co-integration and the vector error correction model

(VECM), he found that about 14 per cent of disequilibrium is corrected every year in the case of "exports of goods and services" and GDP. He also found that the direction of causality was from export growth to GDP growth. He did not find any empirical evidence suggesting a reverse causation. Dash and Parida (2012) examined the role of services exports and services imports in India's economic growth, using a bound-testing approach to an auto-regressive distributed lag (ARDL) model and VECM. Using quarterly data from 1996-97 to 2010-11, they found the existence of a long-run equilibrium relationship between GDP, services exports, services imports and the real effective exchange rate (REER) for the Indian economy. The direction of short-run causality was found to be present only from services exports to GDP, and not vice-versa.

The relationship between the current account balance (CAB) and economic growth has been examined in international theoretical and empirical studies. Brissimis et al. (2010) postulated that a small open economy that starts from a relatively low domestic income is expected to have low savings, as optimal consumption levels are high relative to current income. This implies increased external borrowing against future income, which, coupled with substantial initial investment needs, would translate into a larger current account deficit at early stages of development. As the economy catches up and a higher level of development is achieved, external financing needs tend to moderate. Hence, relative real GDP per capita is expected to be positively related to the current account balance. According to Obstfeld and Rogoff (2007), economies that are in the early stages of development have a greater need for investment and are likely to finance investment through external borrowing. As they develop and approach the income levels of advanced economies, their CAB should improve. Among countries at a similar initial stage of development, the stronger a country's economic growth relative to its trading partners, the lower the current account is likely to be. Hence, theoretically, causality is found to run from economic growth to CAB.

Estimating cross-country regressions for the time span of 1974-2004, Edwards (2007) found that a decline in GDP growth of 1 percentage point relative to the long-term trend resulted in an improvement in the CAB – a higher surplus or lower deficit – of one quarter of a percentage point of GDP. Sekmen and Calisir (2011) examined the trade-off between CAD and economic growth for Turkey for the period from 1998 to 2009. Using VECM and ARDL models, they found the existence of a positive relationship between economic growth and CAD in the short run. However, there have been no Indian empirical studies analysing this relationship.

Mann (2004) proposed two channels through which a rise in new economy services would impact the trajectory of the US current account. First, increased trade in new economy services has improved the income-elasticity asymmetry of US trade. Second, integration of new economy services into the domestic economies of the US's trading partners will raise economic growth there. After estimating new income elasticities for US exports and imports of "new economy services" and incorporating them into a simple model of the US current account, she concluded that reasonable estimates of the above two structural changes are not sufficient to stabilise the US current account deficit, partly because the share of new economy services in US trade is still small. However, these two changes were found to help slow the further widening of the US CAD. Rath and Rajesh (2006) studied the trend in India's services exports and CAD for the post-reform period using descriptive statistics and growth rates. The period of their study was from 1990-91 to 2005-06. They found that the rising surplus in net services exports has been significantly responsible for lower CAD in the Indian economy since the early 1990s.

Data and Methodology

As per IMF's balance of payments framework, the current account balance is defined as the sum of net exports of goods and services, (net) primary income and (net) secondary income. The sum of "investment income" and "compensation of employees" is referred to as primary income. The sum of "private transfers" and "official transfers" is referred to as secondary income. Primary income, secondary income and trade in non-factor services are categorised as "invisibles" in this framework. An in-depth analysis of the contribution of services trade and other invisibles towards India's economic growth and external stabilisation is initially carried out with the help of growth rates, percentage shares etc. This includes an exploration of the accounting relationship between services trade and economic growth in the Indian economy. The time span for the descriptive analysis is the post-reform period, from 1990-91 to 2011-12. A decomposition analysis of the contribution of other invisibles towards the growth in India's national disposable income is also carried out, utilising the methodology used by Jalava and Pohjola (2002).

Thereafter, time-series analysis is used to examine the nature of the relationship between services trade, GDP and current account balance during the post-reform period. Quarterly data [from 1996-97:Q1 to 2011-12:Q4] on all three variables, at current prices, are compiled from "Handbook of Statistics on Indian Economy (2011-12)", published by the

RBI. The year 1996-97 is chosen as the starting point for the time-series analysis, since quarterly data on India's GDP is available only from that particular year. This year is also chosen as the starting point because India's services trade received a boost post-1995 once GATS became operational, facilitated by access to a growing overseas market. All three variables are initially tested for their stationary properties using unit-root tests. In this study, the bound-testing approach to the ARDL model developed by Pesaran et al. (2001) is used to check for the presence of co-integration. This approach is preferred because the direction of causality among the variables is already theoretically known. Moreover, the bound-testing approach can be used regardless of whether the time-series is stationary or integrated to the first order or a mixture of both.

Empirical Results

Contribution of services trade and other invisibles towards external stabilisation

In December 1990, the country was on the brink of a foreign exchange crisis. Forex reserves had depleted to a level that covered only three weeks of imports. India's CAD stood at 2.96 per cent of GDP in 1990-91, and the invisibles balance dipped to Rs.-4.33 billion. RBI had to temporarily pledge gold to raise loans to tide over the crisis. India has come a long way since then on the external front, with the growing contribution of invisibles bringing down India's CAD (Figure 2.1). After 1990-91, invisibles greatly benefited from the economic reforms and the opening up of the Indian economy. India's balance of invisibles, which was Rs.42.59 billion in 1991-92, grew at a CAGR of 25 per cent over the next 20 years, and stood at Rs.3855 billion in 2010-11. India even managed to register a current account surplus for three years (2001-02, 2002-03 and 2003-04) due to a significant surplus in the invisibles account. The invisibles account was in surplus even during the peak of the global economic recession in 2008-09. However, goods trade consistently ran on deficit throughout the study period. The current account balance was bogged down by the widening merchandise trade deficit, because of which India always suffers from a current account deficit.

Figure 2.2 reveals the growth pattern of different components of India's invisibles. It can be safely concluded that the remarkable surplus in India's invisibles balance during the post-reform period can be attributed mainly to workers' remittances (net) and net non-factor services exports. Private transfers more than doubled within a span of one year after the

BoP crisis, from Rs.37.12 billion in 1990-91 to Rs.93.82 billion in 1991-92. Private transfers have grown rapidly ever since, and stood at Rs.3050 billion in 2011-12. India is currently the largest recipient of workers' remittances in the world. Although net non-factor services exports more than doubled from Rs.12.05 billion in 1989-90 to Rs.31.33 billion in 1991-92, they fell during the following years. The major growth spurt in India's trade in non-factor services has been witnessed only in the last decade. Primary income was in deficit throughout the study period, and the contribution of official transfers to the growth in invisibles has been negligible.

Figure 2.3 reveals the growth patterns of different components of India's net non-factor services exports during the post-reform period. It clearly indicates that the spectacular growth witnessed in net exports of non-factor services during the last decade can be attributed to "miscellaneous services". Net exports of miscellaneous services grew at a CAGR of 32 per cent between 2000-01 and 2010-11. Business services, finance and communications, which are categorised as "miscellaneous services" in India's balance of payments, are known worldwide as "new economy services". The contribution of other services towards the growth in net exports of non-factor services was found to be insignificant after 2000.

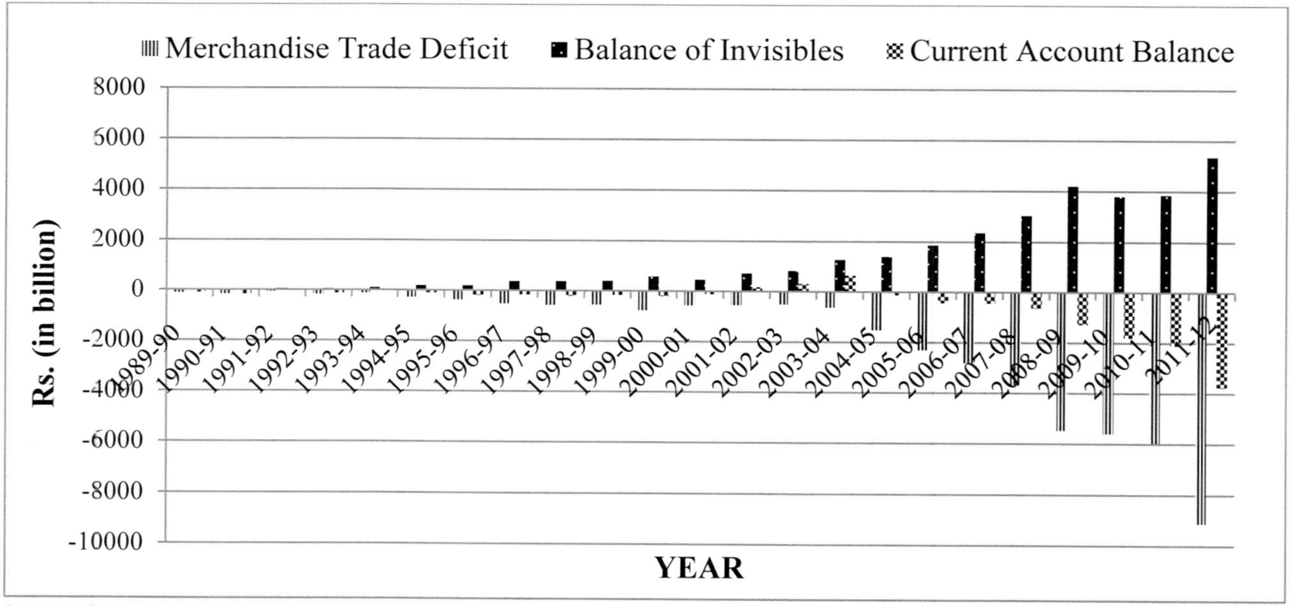

Source: Compiled by author from Handbook of Statistics on Indian Economy 2011-12, RBI

Figure 2.1: India's Current Account Dynamics during the Post-reform Period

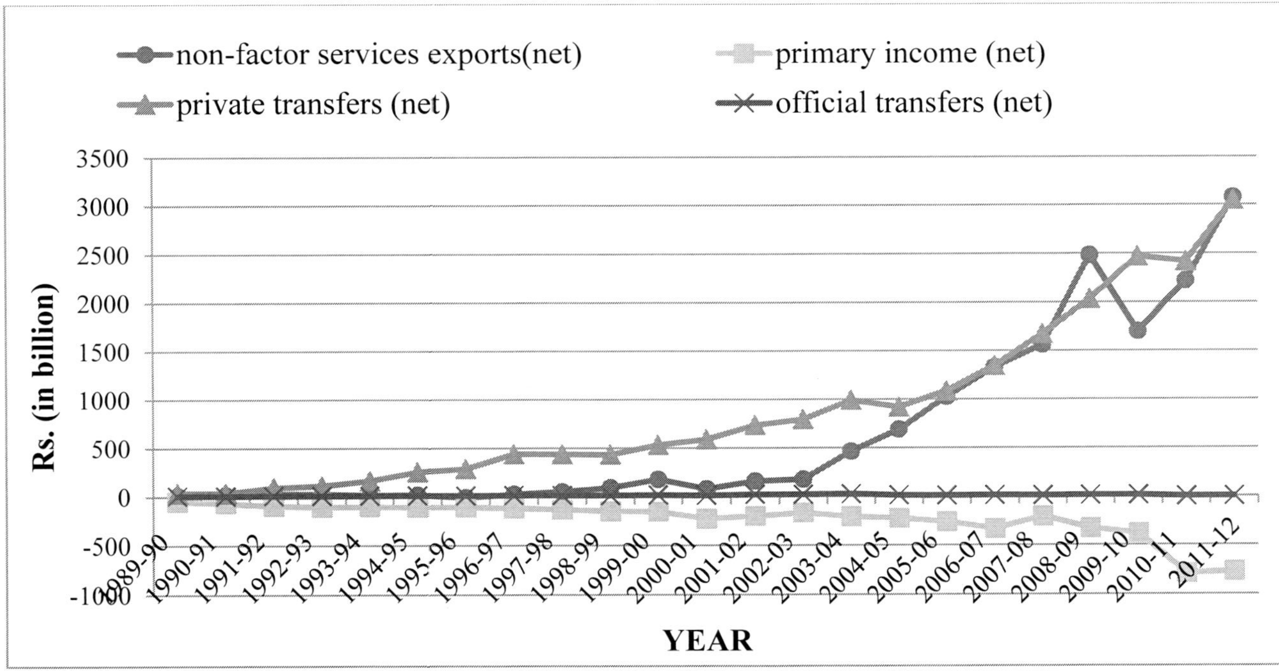

Source: Compiled by author from Handbook of Statistics on Indian Economy 2011-12, RBI

Figure 2.2: Trend in Invisibles in India’s Current Account

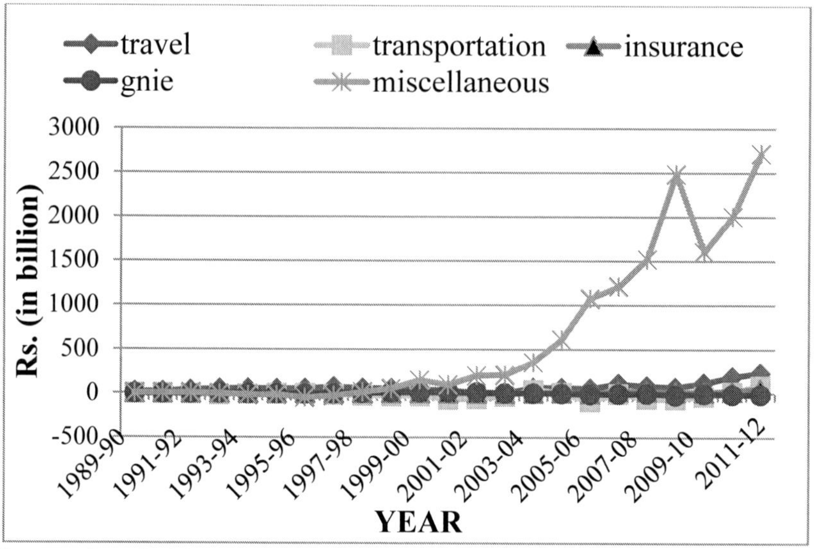

Source: Compiled by author from Handbook of Statistics on Indian Economy (HBSIE) 2011-12, RBI

Figure 2.3: Trends in Different Components of India's Net Exports of Non-factor Services

Table 2.1: Comparing the Contributions of Private Transfers and Net Services Exports towards External Stabilisation

Year	Net Services Exports **	Private transfers (net)**	Current Account Deficit*	CAD without net services Exports *	CAD without private transfers *
1989-90	12.05	37.98	-2.27	-2.5	-3.03
1990-91	17.61	37.12	-2.96	-3.3	-3.6
1991-92	31.33	93.82	-0.3	-0.8	-1.7
1995-96	-7.02	286.6	-1.6	-1.5	-3.9
2000-01	79.05	588.11	-0.5	-0.9	-3.2
2001-02	158.89	733.63	0.7	0.02	-2.4
2002-03	176.44	792.29	1.2	0.5	-1.9

2003-04	463.81	991.65	2.3	0.6	-1.2
2004-05	688.31	919.71	-0.4	-2.5	-3.2
2005-06	1026.11	1085.65	-1.2	-3.96	-4.1
2006-07	1330.64	1346.08	-1.03	-4.1	-4.2
2007-08	1562	1675	-1.3	-4.4	-4.6
2008-09	2484	2032	-2.3	-6.7	-5.9
2009-10	1699	2471	-2.8	-5.4	-6.6
2010-11	2222	2420	-2.7	-5.6	-5.9
2011-12	3079	3050	-4.2	-7.72	-7.69

Source: Author's calculations from Handbook of Statistics on Indian Economy 2011-12, RBI
*Percentage of India's GDP at market prices
**Absolute values in Rs. billion

However, the relevant policy question here is whether private transfers or net services exports have been playing a bigger role in India's external stabilisation. Table 2.1 gives a comparative picture of the inflows from the two sources. It was found that the contribution of private transfers in bringing down India's CAD was higher than that of net services exports during the 1990s, even during the peak of the balance of payments crisis in 1990-91. In the absence of private transfers, the current account surplus that India registered during the years 2001-02, 2002-03 and 2003-04 would have turned into a current account deficit. However, the period since 2004-05 becomes quite crucial when analysing the contribution of net services exports towards India's external stabilisation. The gap in the magnitude of net service exports and private transfers started declining after 2004-05. It was also found that the contribution of private transfers and net services exports in bringing down India's CAD was almost the same during 2005-06 and 2006-07. However, the game-changer was the year 2008-09. During the peak of the global recession in 2008-09, the contribution of net services exports towards India's external stabilisation exceeded that of private transfers. In the absence of net services exports, India's CAD would have been 6.7 per cent of GDP in 2008-09, instead of the actual CAD of 2.3 per cent. In the absence of net private transfers, India's CAD would have been 5.9 per cent of GDP in the same year. Although net services exports dipped in the following years due to the slowdown in developed economies, they recovered and exceeded private transfers in 2011-12.

The interesting finding here is the contrasting behaviour of private transfers and net services exports during the peak of India's balance of payments crisis in 1990-91 and the global economic crisis in 2008-09. Remittances to India were adversely affected during both these years. Remittances, which registered an annual growth rate of 24.4 per cent in 2007-08, declined to 21.3 per cent in 2008-09 in response to the global economic meltdown that year. It was also found that private transfers declined by 2.3 per cent in 1990-91 compared to the previous year. India's international trade in services, on the other hand, has been relatively resilient during the recent economic recession, which was also noted by Borchert and Mattoo (2009). Net services exports registered an annual growth rate of 59 per cent in 2008-09, compared to 17.4 per cent in 2007-08. Most of this can be attributed to India's net exports of miscellaneous services in particular, which registered a spectacular growth in 2008-09 (refer to Figure 2.3). It was also found that net services exports grew by 46 per cent, even in 1990-91, from the previous year. Private transfers, therefore, have been found to be susceptible to being more affected by crises as compared to net exports of non-factor services in the Indian economy.

Accounting relationship between services trade and economic growth

Table 2.2: Percentage Share of Different Components in India's GDP at Market Prices

Year	Final Consumption Expenditure (PFCE+GFCE)	Gross Capital Formation	Merchandise (X-M)	Services (X-M)
1990-91	78.87	24.80	-1.68	0.30
1991-92	79.03	22.56	-0.46	0.46
1992-93	77.51	24.40	-1.08	0.35
1993-94	77.38	21.77	-0.17	0.19
1994-95	75.95	24.14	-0.48	0.18
1995-96	74.94	27.29	-1.10	-0.06
1996-97	75.96	22.70	-1.32	0.18
1997-98	75.57	24.52	-1.53	0.31
1998-99	77.33	23.22	-2.14	0.51
1999-00	78.09	26.75	-2.77	0.88
2000-01	77.17	24.75	-1.26	0.36

2001-02	77.69	24.79	-1.54	0.68
2002-03	75.94	25.83	-1.66	0.70
2003-04	73.87	27.48	-2.32	1.63
2004-05	70.08	32.45	-3.88	2.12
2005-06	69.16	34.28	-5.52	2.78
2006-07	67.99	35.87	-6.26	3.10
2007-08	67.25	38.03	-7.15	3.13
2008-09	68.64	35.53	-9.48	**4.41**
2009-10	69.36	36.41	-8.02	2.63
2010-11	68.29	37.56	-7.04	2.61
2011-12	68.87	35.92	**-10.01**	3.48
Average	**73.86**	**28.68**	**-3.49**	**1.41**

Source: Author's calculations from National Account Statistics, CSO

According to the expenditure approach to national income accounting, GDP at market prices of any country is the sum of consumption, investment and net exports of goods and services. Using this framework, the accounting relationship between economic growth and services trade was examined by separating out net services exports from India's total net exports of goods and services (Table 2.2). For this analysis, annual data on relevant variables compiled from CSO (base year: 2004-05) at current prices (in Rs. crore) were utilised. It was found that the percentage share of net services exports in India's GDP at market prices was negligible throughout the 1990s (at less than 1 per cent). However, the contribution of net services exports was found to be much better than that of net merchandise exports, whose share in India's GDP was negative throughout the post-reform period. The share of net services exports averaged 1.41 per cent for the entire post-reform period, whereas the share of net merchandise exports averaged -3.49 per cent. The share of net services exports in India's GDP crossed 1 per cent in 2003-04; it has been picking up ever since, signifying the growing importance of services trade in India's economic growth during the past decade. The share of net services exports in India's GDP reached a maximum of 4.41 per cent in 2008-09, during the peak of the global economic recession. This can be attributed to the spectacular growth witnessed in miscellaneous services during that particular year. Although the share of net services exports declined in the following two years due to the slowdown in global demand, it recovered again in 2011-12. This empirical analysis points to the potential for services trade to become an engine of export-led growth for the Indian economy in the near future.

Decomposition of the contribution of other invisibles to growth in India's national disposable income

Table 2.3: Decomposition Analysis

Year	Share-weighted growth rate of NDP at Market Prices ($w_1Y_1^\wedge$)	Share-weighted growth rate of NFI from abroad ($w_2Y_2^\wedge$)	Share-weighted growth rate of Remittances (net) from Rest of the World ($w_3Y_3^\wedge$)	Growth rate of India's Net National Disposable Income ($Y^\wedge$)	Contribution of Remittances to Growth in NNDI ($(w_3Y_3^\wedge/w_1Y_1^\wedge + w_2Y_2^\wedge + w_3Y_3^\wedge)$* 100)	Contribution of NFI from abroad to Growth in NNDI ($(w_2Y_2^\wedge/w_1Y_1^\wedge + w_2Y_2^\wedge + w_3Y_3^\wedge)$* 100)
1991-92	14.03	-0.34	4.58	18.27	25.09	-1.84
1992-93	14.49	-0.16	0.59	14.93	3.95	-1.04
1993-94	15.04	-0.04	1.41	16.42	8.61	-0.23
1994-95	17.11	-0.08	1.62	18.64	8.68	-0.45
1995-96	16.87	-0.03	-0.39	16.45	-2.37	-0.19
1996-97	15.37	0.03	2.97	18.37	16.14	0.16
1997-98	10.44	-0.01	-0.01	10.42	-0.13	-0.09
1998-99	14.56	-0.13	-0.04	14.39	-0.25	-0.93
1999-00	11.20	-0.03	0.69	11.86	5.79	-0.26
2000-01	7.19	-0.47	0.32	7.04	4.56	-6.73
2001-02	7.74	0.12	0.74	8.60	8.63	1.36
2002-03	7.33	0.17	0.24	7.74	3.09	2.17
2003-04	12.03	-0.09	0.97	12.91	7.51	-0.72

2004-05	17.73	-0.23	-0.37	17.14	-2.15	-1.32
2005-06	13.66	-0.17	0.54	14.03	3.86	-1.19
2006-07	16.08	-0.27	0.72	16.53	4.35	-1.65
2007-08	15.84	0.38	0.73	16.95	4.32	2.26
2008-09	12.24	-0.61	0.64	12.28	5.21	-4.93
2009-10	14.21	-0.15	0.63	14.69	4.28	-1.03
2010-11	18.95	-1.08	-0.05	17.82	-0.26	-6.07
2011-12	16.67	0.03	0.78	17.48	4.46	0.15
Average	**13.75**	**-0.15**	**0.82**	**14.4**	**5.4**	**-1.07**

Source: Author's calculations from National Account Statistics, CSO

Studying the contribution of other invisibles (except net exports of non-factor services) towards economic growth poses a methodological problem since GDP does not include remittances, compensation of employees or investment income. However, according to national income accounting (NIA), net national disposable income (NNDI) is the sum of (i) net domestic product (NDP) at market prices, (ii) net factor income from abroad and (iii) other current transfers from the rest of the world (net). It needs to be noted here that "net factor income from abroad" in NIA is the sum of "compensation of employees (net)" and "investment income (net)" in the balance of payments. Similarly, "other current transfers from the rest of the world" in NIA is the same as private transfers/remittances in the balance of payments. Therefore, it is possible to quantify the contribution of these invisibles towards the growth in India's national disposable income. For this decomposition analysis, annual data on the relevant variables compiled from CSO (base year: 2004-05) at current prices (in Rs. crore) were utilised. Accordingly, the growth rate of India's NNDI ($Y^{\wedge}$) is decomposed to the sum of (i) the share-weighted growth rate of India's NDP at market prices ($w_1Y_1^{\wedge}$), (ii) the share-weighted growth rate of net factor income (NFI) from abroad ($w_2Y_2^{\wedge}$) and (iii) the share-weighted growth rate of other current transfers (net) from the rest of the world ($w_3Y_3^{\wedge}$). Here, the weights w_1, w_2 and w_3 give the respective shares of the three components in India's total NNDI.

$$Y^{\wedge} = w_1Y_1^{\wedge} + w_2Y_2^{\wedge} + w_3Y_3^{\wedge} \quad ; \quad w_1+w_2+w_3 = 1$$

The average share of NDP at market prices in India's NNDI was found to be $w_1 = 0.98$; the average share of "net factor income from abroad" in India's NNDI was found to be $w_2 = -0.01$, and the average share of "other current transfers (net) from the rest of the world" in India's NNDI was found to be $w_3 = 0.03$. The annual growth rates of these three components ($Y_1^{\wedge}$, $Y_2^{\wedge}$, $Y_3^{\wedge}$) were also computed. The growth rate of India's NNDI averaged 14.4 per cent during the study period (Table 2.3). It was found that growth in remittances is the only component among "other invisibles" that contributed to the growth of the country's national disposable income in the post-reform period. The contribution of remittances to growth in NNDI remained below 10 per cent for most years, except 1991-92 and 1996-97. The impressive contribution of about 25 per cent in 1991-92 can mostly be attributed to the great surge in remittances after India's forex crisis of 1990-91. The contribution of remittances to growth in NNDI averaged 5.4 per cent during the study period. The contribution of compensation of employees and investment income to growth in NNDI remained negligible and negative for most of the study period, and averaged -1.07 per cent. The contribution of remittances to growth in NDI was also negative during five years of the period covered in the study.

Time-series Analysis

The macroeconomic variables, current account balance (CAB), GDP at market prices, and net services exports are initially examined for their unit-root properties. The results of the ADF and KPSS tests are reported in Tables A1 and A2 in the Appendix 2.1. All three variables are found to be I(1), i.e. integrated of order 1. This implies that the data series is non-stationary at levels, and becomes stationary only at first difference. During the literature review, economic growth and services trade were found to influence the behaviour of the current account balance. Therefore, the bound-testing approach to the ARDL model was used to check for the presence of any co-integrating relationship among these variables. One significant advantage of this approach over other co-integration techniques is that different variables can be assigned different lag-lengths in the ARDL model. The model has been specified in the linear form since it is not possible to derive the logarithmic form for CAB and net services exports, because these variables take on positive as well as negative values.

$$\Delta CAB_t = \alpha_0 + \sum \beta_{1i}\, \Delta CAB_{t-i} + \sum \beta_{2j}\, \Delta GDP_{t-j} + \sum \beta_{3k}\, \Delta ServX\_M_{t-k} + \beta_4\, CAB_{t-1} + \beta_5\, GDP_{t-1} + \beta_6\, ServX\_M_{t-1} + u_t$$

The existence of a co-integrated relationship between the variables in the above ARDL model specification is examined with the help of F or Wald test statistics. The Wald test examines the joint null hypothesis of zero co-integration between the variables (H_0: $\beta_4=\beta_5=\beta_6=0$) against the alternate hypothesis of the presence of co-integration. The calculated F-statistics are compared with two sets of critical values computed by Pesaran et al. (2001) for a given level of significance in their bound-testing approach to the analysis of long-run relationships. If the computed F-statistic exceeds the upper critical bound value, it implies that all the variables are I(1) and the null hypothesis of zero co-integration can be rejected. If the computed F-statistic is below the lower critical bounds value, it implies that all variables are I(0) and the null hypothesis of zero co-integration cannot be rejected. However, if the calculated F-statistic falls within the bounds, then the test becomes inconclusive.

Table 2.4: ARDL (3,1,2) Model Estimation Results

Dependent Variable: D(CA_BAL)				
Included observations: 60 after adjustments				
Variable	**Coefficient**	**Std. Error**	**t-Statistic**	**Prob.**
C	171.44	78.49	2.18	0.03
D(CA_BAL(-1))	-0.29	0.19	-1.49	0.14
D(CA_BAL(-2))	-0.33	0.16	-2.02	0.05
D(CA_BAL(-3))	-0.22	0.14	-1.55	0.13
D(GDPMP(-1))	0.09	0.03	2.67	0.01
D(SERV_X_M(-1))	-0.29	0.31	-0.93	0.36
D(SERV_X_M(-2))	0.57	0.29	1.93	0.06
CA_BAL(-1)	-0.31	0.19	-1.61	0.11
GDPMP(-1)	-0.03	0.01	-2.15	0.04
SERV_X_M(-1)	0.09	0.26	0.33	0.75
R-squared	0.51	Mean dependent var.		-18.21
Adjusted R-squared	0.43	S.D. dependent var.		197.26
S.E. of regression	149.42	Akaike info criterion		13.002
Sum squared resid	1116379.	Schwarz criterion		13.35
Log likelihood	-380.07	Hannan-Quinn criter.		13.14
F-statistic	5.87	Durbin-Watson stat.		1.95
Prob (F-statistic)	0.000015			

Source: Author's calculations
Note: Lag-length was chosen on the basis of AIC

Table 2.4 gives the estimation results for the ARDL (3,1,2) model. When the Wald test was done for this model, the F-statistic was found to be 5.29 (with p value = 0.0030). The Wald test results are given in Table A3 in the Appendix 2.1. Assuming a model with unrestricted intercept and no trend, and with two regressors (k=2), the lower and upper bound values of the F-statistic from Pesaran et al. (2001) are 3.79 and 4.85 at the 5 per cent level of significance. Since the computed F-statistic exceeds the critical upper bound at the 5 per cent significance level, the null hypothesis of zero co-integration can be rejected in this case. This establishes the presence of a long-run equilibrium relationship between current account balance, GDP and net services exports for the Indian economy during the post-reform period. Furthermore, the long-run coefficient for GDP was found to be negative and significant, implying that an increase in GDP leads to a deterioration in CAB. This implies that India still has not reached the stage of developed economies when the needs of economic growth do not take a toll on a country's CAB. In the case of a developing country like India, this inverse relationship can be explained in terms of rising energy demand, which is a major factor behind the increasing import bill. The long-run coefficient for net services exports was found to be positive but insignificant, implying that an increase in net services exports leads to an improvement in CAB. This is in consensus with the findings of Mann (2004) for the US economy.

The Granger Representation Theorem states that if a set of variables are co-integrated, then there exists a valid error correction representation of the data. Hence, a vector error correction model was estimated to study the short-run dynamics. The error correction term (ECT) in the VECM was found to be negative and statistically significant at the 5 per cent level, reaffirming the earlier finding of the existence of a co-integrated relationship among the variables. The ECT was found to be -0.48, implying that about 48 per cent of the short-run disequilibrium between net services exports, GDP and CAB is corrected every quarter. A key assumption in this bound-testing methodology is that the errors of the estimated ARDL model must be serially independent. Hence, diagnostic tests were performed on the estimated model and the test results are given in Table A4 and A5 in the Appendix 2.1. It was found that the estimated ARDL model suffers from neither autocorrelation nor heteroscedasticity.

Conclusion and Policy Implications

The quantum, quality and financing of CAD have recently emerged as major concerns for Indian policy makers, faced with a gloomy macro-economic scenario of decelerating growth, large-scale capital exit from stock markets and massive rupee depreciation. The IMF's approach to external stabilisation often involves a reduction in CAD by introducing deep cuts in domestic investment, which is not a good recipe for economic growth. Moreover, gold and oil imports, which largely account for India's burgeoning CAD, have been found to be relatively inelastic to income changes. In this context, this paper finds the existence of a long-run equilibrium relationship between net services exports, GDP and current account balance in the Indian economy during the post-reform period. This paper also finds that private transfers were more crisis-prone than net services exports. Hence, this paper argues for a bigger role for net services exports in bringing down India's CAD, rather than remittances. Moreover, some of the remittances are likely to filter out of the economy via higher imports of goods and services. Therefore, the net impact on the current account balance maybe much smaller than the actual flow of remittances.

However, the contribution of remittances to the growth in India's national disposable income is duly noted. Although India is a significant player in the world market for services, most of the world trade in services still takes place between developed countries. Adopting policies that promote and diversify India's services exports and export markets and raise India's export competitiveness in the world services market is a much better recipe for India's external stabilisation.

References

Balassa, Bela. 1978. "Exports and Economic Growth: Further Evidence." *Journal of Development Economics* 5 (2): 181-89.

Beckerman, Wilfred. 1965. "Demand, Exports and Growth." In *The Britain Economy in 1975*, edited by W. Beckerman and Associates, 44-72. UK: Cambridge University Press.

Bhagwati, Jagdish. 1988. *Protectionism.* Cambridge: MIT Press.

Borchert, Ingo, and Aaditya Mattoo. 2009. "The Crisis Resilience of Services Trade." Policy Research Working Paper 4917, World Bank, Washington DC.

Brissimis, Sophocles N., George Hondroyiannis, Christos Papazoglou, Nicholas T. Tsaveas and Melina A. Vasardani. 2010. "Current Account Determinants and External Sustainability in Periods of Structural Change." Working Paper Series 1243, European Central Bank, Frankfurt am Main.

Dash, Ranjan K., and Purna C. Parida. 2012. "Services Trade and Economic Growth in India: An Analysis in the Post-reform Period." *International Journal of Economics and Business Research* 4 (3): 326-45.

Edwards, Sebastian. 2007. "On Current Account Surpluses and the Correction of Global Imbalances." NBER Working Paper 12904, National Bureau of Economic Research, Cambridge, MA.

Feder, Gershon. 1982. "On Exports and Economic Growth." *Journal of Development Economics* 12 (1-2): 59-73.

GOI (Government of India). 2011. *Faster, Sustainable and More Inclusive Growth: An Approach to the Twelfth Five Year Plan (2012-17).* New Delhi: Planning Commission.

—. 2012. *Economic Survey 2011-12*. New Delhi: Ministry of Finance.

Goyal, Ashima. 2012. "Causes and Cures for India's Current Account Deficit." *Hindu Businessline*, August 8.

Goyal, Rajan. 2012. "Sustainable Level of India's Current Account Deficit." RBI Working Paper Series 16, Reserve Bank of India, Mumbai.

Grossman, Gene M., and Elhanan Helpman. 1991. *Innovation and Growth in the Global Economy*. Cambridge: MIT Press.

Jalava, Jukka, and Matti Pohjola. 2002. "Economic Growth in the New Economy: Evidence from Advanced Economies." *Information Economics and Policy* 14: 189-210.

Krugman, Paul. 1984. "Import Protection as Export Promotion: International Competition in the Presence of Oligopoly and Economies of Scale." In *Monopolistic Competition in International Trade*, edited by H. Kierkowski. Oxford: Oxford University Press.

Lee, Jong W. 1995. "Capital Goods Imports and Long-run Growth." *Journal of Development Economics* 48 (1): 91-110.

Mann, Catherine L. 2002. "Perspectives on the U.S. Current Account Deficit and Sustainability." *Journal of Economic Perspectives* 16 (3): 131-52.

—. 2004. "The U.S. Current Account, New Economy Services, and Implications for Sustainability." *Review of International Economics* 12 (2): 262-276.

Obstfeld, Maurice, and Kenneth Rogoff. 2007. *Foundations of International Macroeconomics*. Cambridge: MIT Press.

Oulton, Nicholas. 2001. "Must the Growth Rate Decline? Baumol's Unbalanced Growth Revisited." *Oxford Economic Papers* 53 (4): 605-27.

Pesaran, Hashem M., Yongcheol Shin and Richard J. Smith. 2001. "Bound Testing Approaches to the Analysis of Level Relationships." *Journal of Applied Econometrics* 16: 289-326.

Pradhan, Narayan C. 2010. "Exports and Economic Growth: An Examination of ELG Hypothesis for India." *Reserve Bank of India Occasional Papers* 31 (3): 35-66.

Rath, Deba P., and Raj Rajesh. 2006. "Analytics and Implications of Services Sector Growth in Indian Economy." *The Journal of Income and Wealth* 28 (1): 1-20.

Sekmen, Fuat, and Mustafa Calisir. 2011. "Is there a Trade-off between Current Account Deficits and Economic Growth? The Case of Turkey." *International Research Journal of Finance and Economics* 62: 166-72.

UNCTAD (United Nations Conference on Trade and Development). 2013. *Trade and Development Report 2013*. Geneva: United Nations.

Vernon, Raymond. 1966. "International Investment and International Trade in the Product Cycle." *Quarterly Journal of Economics* 80 (2): 190-207.

WTO (World Trade Organisation). 2012. *World Trade Report 2012*. Geneva: WTO.

Appendix 2.1

Table A1: Testing for Stationarity - ADF test

variable	**test statistic**	**Lag**	**test statistic**	**Lag**	**test statistic**	**lag**	**test statistic**	**Lag**
	(level)		(level)		First Difference		First difference	
	Intercept		Intercept + trend		Intercept		Intercept + trend	
GDPMP	3.34	5	1.796	5	-4.27*	2	-20.7*	2
CAB	1.72	3	0.127	3	-8.12*	2	-8.78*	2
Serv (X-M)	0.0028	1	-2.517	1	-9.15*	0	-9.33*	0

*The **null hypothesis** that the variable concerned is **non-stationary** can be rejected at 1% significance level

Table A2: Testing for Stationarity - KPSS test

variable	test statistic	test statistic	test statistic	test statistic
	(level)	(level)	(First difference)	(First difference)
	Intercept	Intercept + Trend	Intercept	Intercept + trend
GDPMP	0.95*	0.25*	0.38	0.14
CAB	0.79*	0.28*	0.402	0.14
Serv(X-M)	0.96*	0.23*	0.33	0.08

*The **null hypothesis** that the variable concerned is **stationary** can be rejected at 1% significance level

Table A3: Wald Test for ARDL Model

Test Statistic	Value	df	Probability
F-statistic	5.291353	(3, 50)	0.0030
Chi-square	15.87406	3	0.0012
Joint Null Hypothesis: C(8)=C(9)=C(10)=0			
Normalised Restriction (= 0)		Value	Std. Err.
C(8)		-0.312765	0.193766
C(9)		-0.030397	0.014159
C(10)		0.086079	0.263217

Table A4: Testing for Autocorrelation in ARDL model: Breush-Godfrey LM Test

Lags	F-Stat	Prob.(F)	Obs*R-squared	Prob.(Chi-square)
1*	0.00066	0.98	0.00081	0.98
2*	0.14453	0.87	0.35916	0.84
3*	0.51511	0.67	1.90997	0.59
4*	0.41262	0.79	2.07823	0.72
Null H_0: no serial correlation at lag order p*				

*The null hypothesis cannot be rejected at the 1% significance level.

Table A5: Testing for Heteroscedasticity in ARDL model: White Test

F-Stat	Prob.(F)	Obs*R-squared	Prob.(Chi-square)
1.41711	0.21	12.19425	0.20

*The null hypothesis of homoscedasticity cannot be rejected at the 1% significance level.

CHAPTER THREE

STRUCTURAL CHANGE AND CYCLES IN TRADE IN SERVICES: EVIDENCE FROM INDIA

C.T. VIDYA

This study empirically analyses the growth and cycles of India's trade in services for the period 1950-2010. Using the Lee and Strazicich's structural break test, the study tests whether the growth in trade in services has evolved gradually over time or whether this was in response to policy changes. The structural break test used in this study does not reveal any significant breaks in services exports and imports. Hence, the study finds that the growth in services trade evolved gradually over the years. Further, the study also addresses the question of whether the integration of the services sector with the rest of the world has paved the way for the transmission of external cyclical upturns and downturns to India. The study identifies three cycles during the period 1950-2010: the first one from 1963-64 to 1981-82; the second from 1981-82 to 1999-2000 and the third with a short peak in the post-2000 period. Moreover, it finds that services exports propel cycles, as shocks in exports exhibit a higher intensity than those in imports.

Introduction

In recent years, the services sector in India has exhibited a high growth trajectory. The contribution of the services sector to the country's GDP has increased from 40 per cent in 1990-91 to 60 per cent in 2010-11. Furthermore, India's services sector exports have also increased, from USD 8 billion to USD 308 billion during the same period. More importantly, India has become the 10th largest services exporter in the world and the second largest exporter of computer and information technology services (GO1, 2010-11). Moreover, the services sector plays an important role in the growth of the Indian economy by linking production blocks across geographically dispersed economic activities. This has led to the internationalisation of services, which in turn has paved the way for technology transfers, the digitisation of the sector and transition towards new characteristics such as transportability and storability.[1]

In addition to this, it must be noted that changes in world demand and the pattern of world trade also have affected India's services trade. Thus, domestic policy changes and external demand variations affect the trade performance of the sector and, in turn, the growth of the economy. This assumes significance as trade in services has emerged as a global growth driver in recent times. On this premise, some studies[2] have argued that favourable policy measures, an increased role in GATS and emphasis on specialisation have enhanced India's services trade. Given that trade in services has grown over the years, the first objective of this chapter is to examine whether trade evolved gradually over the period in question or changed abruptly in response to policy changes. We utilise the structural break test to determine the existence of any breaks in trade in services. This, in turn, helps to characterise distinct and unique phases in the growth of trade in services. For instance, it may be argued that a gradual evolution of trade in services would have resulted from integration with world markets. Moreover, it is possible that shocks originating elsewhere could get transmitted to India's services sector. In the light of these assumptions, we also attempt to identify the cycles in trade in services that occur due to the oscillations or recurring shocks emanating from greater economic integration. Before addressing these issues empirically, a brief description of the growth in India's services trade is given in the following section.

Growth of India's trade in services

The growth of India's trade in services from 1950 to 2010 is analysed using aggregate growth trends as well as component-wise growth. The overall time period is divided into three sub-periods: 1950-1975; 1976-1991 and 1992-2010. This periodisation is carried out in accordance with the changing importance of services in the economy. It is argued that the first growth spurt in the economy occurred in 1975, making it a suitable cut off year to analyse trade performance (Basu, 2007; Panagariya, 2008). The second period (1976-1991) can be described as the era in which the services sector had a substantial share in the total output and employment

[1] Thus, the assumption of direct proximity between producer and consumer has become redundant (Mizzo and Soete, 2001).

[2] See for details Chanda (2009, 2011); Banga (2005).

of the economy, with the year 1991 indicating changes in the policy regime. The third period (1992-2010) can be referred to as the reform period, with the economy undergoing changes in the policy environment.

It can be seen from Table 3.1 that both exports and imports of services rose substantially after 1975 compared to the previous decades. The average annual growth rate of services exports increased from 9 per cent in 1950-1975 to 22 per cent in 1976-1991, and to 24 per cent for the next period, 1992-2010. Simultaneously, the average annual growth rate in imports, which was around 7.4 per cent in 1950-1975, increased to 21.9 per cent in 1976-1991 and 22.8 per cent in the next period, 1992-2010. Furthermore, Table 3.1 also shows the component-wise trend of services trade. For instance, the annual average growth of travel services registered the highest rate of growth at 16.7 per cent, followed by government not included elsewhere (GNIE) with 13 per cent, transport services with 9.6 per cent and miscellaneous services recording 6.6 per cent during 1950-1975. In the case of imports, transport demonstrated the highest growth with 14.9 per cent, followed by insurance services at 8.9 per cent and the miscellaneous sector at 8.4 per cent during the same period.

Table 3.1: Annual Average Growth Rate of Services Exports and Imports

Service Sector	Services Exports			Services Imports		
	1950-1975	1976-1991	1992-2010	1950-975	1976-1991	1992-2010
Transport	9.6	17.9	20.7	14.9	20.4	23.0
Travel	16.7	32.4	18.8	1.9	28.7	26.7
Insurance	6.3	18.3	23.3	8.9	22.2	27.3
GNIE	13.0	8.7	71.9	4.8	20.1	19.8
Miscellaneous	6.6	28.7	25.7	8.4	26.1	27.2
Total	9.0	22.2	24	7.4	21.9	22.8

Source: Calculated from Handbook of Statistics on Indian Economy, RBI (various years)

The next period, 1976 to 1991, was a transitional phase for the export of services. Travel services still dominated, but there was a deceleration in the growth rate of GNIE. However, the miscellaneous sector outpaced the rest of the components with a high growth rate of 28 per cent. Thus, this period saw the miscellaneous sector emerging as a major growth-inducing sector.

Similarly, changes can be observed in the growth composition of imports. Travel services registered the highest growth, with an annual average of 28.7 per cent, closely followed by miscellaneous services, with 26 per cent.

The period of 1992-2010 also shows a remarkable shift in the growth composition. GNIE, which registered a low growth rate compared to other sectors in the previous decades, emerged as the dominant sector, with a growth of 71.9 per cent, whereas there was a marginal decline in the growth of the miscellaneous sector, to 25.7 per cent. A probable reason is the impact of the global financial crisis during 2008-2009.[3] A sudden spurt in the growth of GNIE was seen in 1996-97, which could be due to a steep rise in receipts (expenses from foreign embassies in India) during 1996. There was also a huge increase in GNIE receipts in the other category.[4] The other category, which had a meagre share of Rs.13 crore in 1995-96, had risen to Rs.181 crore in 1996-97.

It is discernible from Table 3.2 that the share of GNIE receipts in total services export has remained at less than 1 per cent. On the other hand, the percentage share of the miscellaneous sector in total services exports shows an unprecedented rise. The miscellaneous sector can be further divided into software services and non-software services. The percentage contribution of software services has risen from 39 per cent in 2000-2001 to 45.5 per cent in 2008-2009, while non-software services averages around 28 per cent for the period from 1992 to 2009.

An analysis of growth periodisation carried out on services trade reveals that both exports and imports showed a significant rise after 1975. A visible change in the growth path of trade in services took place, especially after 1975. It was in the latter half of the 1970s that traditional (personal) services were outpaced by new and emerging services such as software and other miscellaneous sectors. The impetus could be due to domestic deregulation measures and subsequent liberalisation initiatives through GATS. Therefore, it is important to analyse whether the growth in trade in service evolved gradually over the period or whether it was in response to policy changes. Gradual evolution is possibly linked to the integration of the Indian economy with global markets. Another consequence of the integration of the Indian economy with the rest of the world is the transmission of trade fluctuations elsewhere in the world. These shocks, in turn, generate fluctuations in India's trade in services.

In the Indian context, increased attention has been devoted to examining structural breaks in macroeconomic series and not specifically

---

[3] This year marked a negative growth in exports.

[4] The composition of 'other category' receipts is not reported in RBI published sources (Monthly RBI bulletin, 1990).

in the volume of trade. Studies such as those by Ghatak (1996), Ghosh (1999) and most recently, Balakrishnan and Parameshwaran (2007) used the structural break test to identify the growth phases of output and its components. However, there is a dearth of studies on structural changes in India's services trade. The same is true for analysing cycles. Most studies, including those by Chitre (1982), Dua and Banerji (1999, 2007) and Paul (2010), have analysed business cycles by taking into account fluctuations in macroeconomic aggregates and commodity trade. There is not much work on understanding business cycles in the services sector. Given the growing integration of the Indian economy with rest of the world and the increasing dominance of the services sector, it is important to analyse the transmission of cycles by identifying their turning points.

Table 3.2: Composition of India's Services Exports (Receipts)

Year	Travel Services	Transport Services	Insurance Services	GNIE Services	Miscellaneous Sector		Total Services
					Software Services	Non-software Services*	
1990-91	32	21.6	2.4	0.3	-	43.6	100
1995-96	36.9	27.4	2.4	0.2	-	33.1	100
2000-01	21.5	12.6	1.7	4	39	21.3	100
2001-02	18.3	12.6	1.7	3	44.1	20.3	100
2002-03	16	12.2	1.8	1.4	46.2	22.4	100
2003-04	18.7	11.9	1.6	0.9	47.6	19.2	100
2004-05	15.4	10.8	2	0.9	40.9	29.9	100
2005-06	13.6	11	1.8	0.5	40.9	32.1	100
2006-07	12.4	10.8	1.6	0.3	42.4	32.4	100
2007-08	12.6	11.1	1.8	0.4	44.6	29.6	100
2008-09	10.7	11.1	1.4	0.4	45.5	30.9	100

Note: *include Business and Personal Services
Source: RBI Monthly Bulletin (2010)

Data and Methodology

In order to test structural breaks and business cycles in trade in services and its components, annual data from 1950 to 2010 is used. Most of the data are collected from the Handbook of Statistics on Indian Economy published by the RBI. To test a structural break, we use unit root tests, such as the Phillips-Perron (hereafter PP), and the multiple break test (hereafter LM) proposed by Lee and Strazicich (2003). The structural break test is discussed in Appendix 3.1. Similarly, for cycles, the Hodrick and Prescott filter method is applied to decompose the time series data into cycles, trends and irregular shocks. A brief discussion on the Hodrick and Prescott filter method is presented in Appendix 3.2.

Empirical Results

Structural breaks in trade in services

The empirical analysis is carried out in two steps. First, the conventional unit root test by Phillips-Perron is performed for trade in services and its components to establish the order of integration. The intent of this exercise is to check whether the variables are stationary or not. In the second step, the LM test for multiple structural breaks is performed on the above series to test for structural breaks. Table 3.3 presents the results of the PP unit root test.

The results show that the null hypothesis of stationarity is rejected in levels for all variables and accepted in first differences. This indicates that exports, imports and their components are non-stationary or I(1) in levels. To identify the structural breaks, we apply the LM unit test to aggregated and disaggregated exports and imports and the results are given in Table 3.4. The results show that the test statistics corresponding to SX and SM are less than the critical values given in Table 3.5, implying that there is no structural break in aggregate service exports and imports. The only break years found significant in the LM test were for travel and GNIE.

Disaggregated services exports show a slightly different picture compared to imports. The only sector which registered a significant structural break (LM) is the GNIE, which had break years during 1988 and 1998. Further, export trend breaks are not related to import trend breaks, implying that structural breaks do not have a strong relationship with the extent of growth in trade in services.

These indications provide some vital clues on the importance of sector-wise growth to the overall performance of trade in services. First, it can be inferred that growth in services trade has evolved gradually over the years.

That is, it has not changed abruptly, nor does it display a change in relation to various policy regimes initiated in the economy. This gradual evolution is possibly linked to the gradual integration of the Indian economy with global markets.

Another consequence of the integration of the Indian economy with the rest of the world is the impact of trade fluctuations elsewhere in the world. These shocks could generate fluctuations in India's trade in services.

Table 3.3: Unit-Root Tests for Trade in Services Variables, India, 1950-2010

Series	pp unit	Test type	Lag	t-stat	Order of Integration
Services Exports	Level	With intercept	4	2.744	I(1)
	FD		4	-6.091*	I(0)
a) Travel	Level	With intercept	4	-0.034	I(1)
	FD			-5.655*	I(0)
b) Transport	Level	With intercept	4	2.487	I(1)
	FD			-6.536*	I(0)
c) Insurance	Level	With intercept	4	3.062	I(1)
	FD			-7.644*	I(0)
d) GNIE	Level	With intercept	4	-1.146	I(1)
	FD			-5.739*	I(0)
e) Miscellaneous	Level	With intercept	4	2.217	I(1)
	FD			-6.620*	I(0)
Services Imports	Level	With intercept	4	2.963	I(1)
	FD			-7.203*	I(0)
a) Travel	Level	With intercept	4	2.191	I(1)
	FD			-7.362*	I(0)
b) Transport	Level	With intercept	4	2.191	I(1)
	FD			-8.097*	I(0)
c) Insurance	Level	With intercept	4	1.329	I(1)
	FD			-8.288*	I(0)
d) GNIE	Level	With intercept	4	0.642	I(1)
	FD			-9.933*	I(0)
e) Miscellaneous	Level	With intercept	4	2.258	I(1)
	FD			-5.673*	I(0

Notes: FD denotes first difference, * denotes rejection of a unit root at 1%

Table 3.4: Two Break Minimum LM Unit Root Test

Series	Lag	TB	Test Statistic	Critical values of break points
SX	1	1974, 1987	-4.846	λ= (0.37, 06)
SM	1	1970, 1994	-5.157	λ= (0.31, 0.72)
Disaggregated Services Exports				
GNIE	1	1988, 1998	-6.969*	λ= (0.62, 0.79)
Travel	1	1964, 1977	-4.647	λ= (0.2, 0.43)
Transport	1	1968, 1988	-3.842	λ= (0.27, 0.62)
Insurance	1	1965 1990	-4.781	λ= (0.22, 0.65)
Miscellaneous	1	1968, 2000	-3.857	λ= (0.27, 0.82)
Disaggregated Services Imports				
GNIE	1	1976, 1994	5.7047**	λ= (0.41, 0.74)
Travel	1	1977, 1997	-5.043	λ= (0.43, 0.93)
Transport	1	1964, 1991	5.6201***	λ= (0.20, 0.67)
Insurance	1	1963, 1985	-4.539	λ= (0.18,0.56)
Miscellaneous	1	1976, 1993	-5.081	λ= (0.41, 0,70)

Notes: TB denotes the estimated break points. Critical values are shown below for the two-break minimum LM unit root test with linear trend (Model C) at the 1%, 5%, and 10% levels for a sample of size T = 100, respectively. The critical values depend (somewhat) on the location of the breaks λ= (TB1/T, TB2/T) and are symmetric around λ and (1- λ). *, **. *** denote statistical significance at 1%, 5% and 10% respectively

Table 3.5: Critical Values for LM Test

Break points	Critical values		
λ= (TB1/T, TB2/T)	1%	5%	10%
λ= (0.2, 0.4)	-6.16	-5.59	-5.27
λ= (0.2, 0.6)	-6.41	-5.74	-5.32
λ= (0.2, 0.8)	-6.33	-5.71	-5.33
λ= (0.4, 0.6)	-6.45	-5.67	-5.31
λ= (0.4, 0.8)	-6.42	-5.65	-5.32
λ= (0.6, 0.8)	-6.32	-5.73	-5.32

Source: Lee and Strazicich (2003, 2004)

Cycles in trade in services

The cyclical component (C_t) of trade in services derived from the HP filter method is shown in Figure 3.1. This cyclical series can be considered a business cycle in trade in services. It can be seen from the figure that there were three cycles in the sector during the period 1950-2010: one during 1963-64 to 1981-82; a second one during 1981-82 to 1999-2000 and a third after 2000. Table 3.6 gives a time frame of the phases of the cycles in trade in services.

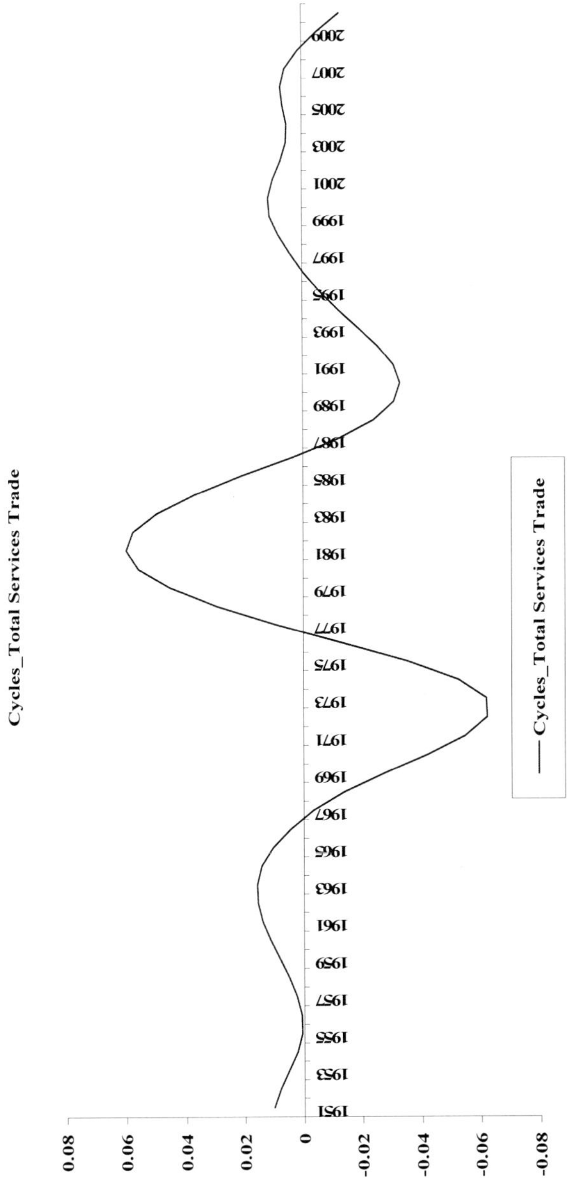

Figure 3.1: Cycles in Trade in Services

Table 3.6: Cycles in Trade in Services

	1st Cycle	2nd Cycle
Peak	1962-63	1981-82
Recession	1967-68 to 1972-73	1987-88 to 1989-90
Trough	1972-73	1989-90
Recovery	1977-78 to 1981-82	1997-98 to 2006-07

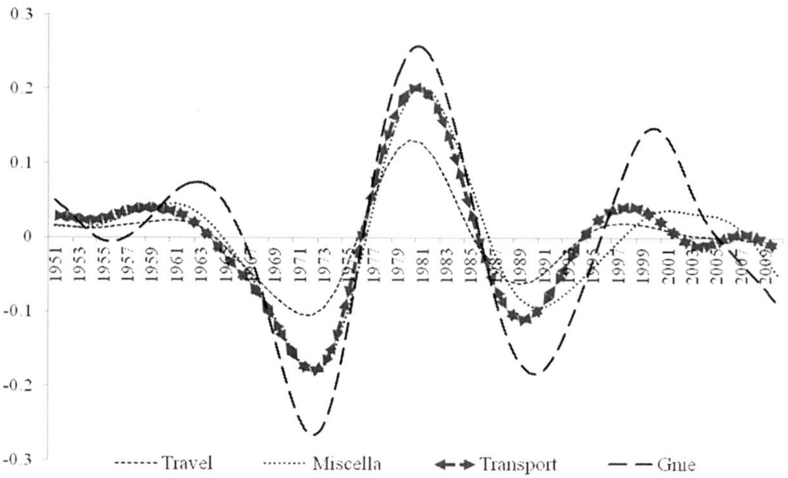

Figure 3.2: Cycles in Dis-aggregated Components of Services Trade

First Cycle (1963-64 to 1981-82)

The first cycle began with a peak in 1962-63 and entered a period of recession from 1967 to 1973, finally reaching a trough during 1972-73. It then recovered in the year 1977 and attained another peak in 1981-82. It can be deduced that the cyclical intensity of sub-sectors has a considerable role to play in the determination and causes of service trade cycles. The reason for the initial boom in 1962-63 can be attributed to the performance of the GNIE sector, which registered the highest peak in the same year (Figure 3.2). The comparatively good performance of GNIE services may have been due to high diplomatic expenditure and expenditure on international agencies (Mukherjee, 1983). Further, the high peak can also be attributed to the government initiative to attract foreign investment for the first time in the third five-year plan (Panagariya, 2008).

It can be seen from Figure 3.2 that all sectors experienced a downturn during 1972-73. GNIE registered the highest downfall during the period. This is also a period in which the Indian economy faced two years of droughts, in 1971-72 and 1972-73, and the first oil price shocks, inflation and economic stagnation. Towards the end of 1977-78, the sector entered the recovery stage, which lasted until 1981-82. The recovery period could be attributed to the transport and miscellaneous category along with GNIE. The rapid growth of the transportation sector during the late 1970s can be explained by two phenomena: increased merchandise exports and a rapid growth in Indian shipping. An increase in the number of tourists from the West Asian countries also resulted in an increase in travel receipts. The growth in the miscellaneous sector was because of greater import of technical know-how and foreign collaborations and a rise in royalty payments and payments for technical and professional services, management fees, office expenses and advertisement charges (Mukherjee, 1983).

Second Cycle (1981-82 to 1997-2006)

The second cycle, which began with the peak of 1981-82 and entered the recessionary phase during the period from 1987 to 1990, finally reached a trough during 1989-1990 and subsequently recovered in the year 1997 to attain another short peak during 2000, after which it followed a similar trend till 2007. The short peak of 2000 cannot be considered another, third cycle. The reasons for this are that (i) the amplitude is too small to measure and (ii) the cycle is still ongoing and hence cannot be evaluated.

Short cycle (2000 -ongoing)

The service trade has been going through a period of recession since 2000, due to a steep fall in GNIE and negative growth in the remaining sectors. It can be seen that the intensity of recession was much lower for travel, transport and miscellaneous sectors, while GNIE showed the highest decline. The deceleration in GNIE may be due to a reduction in foreign embassy expenditures in India and to a decline in imports. Another possible reason is that the Indian economy was also experiencing a period of recession due to the balance of payments (BoP) crisis in 1991, caused by a rise in oil prices, current account deficit, inflationary pressure etc.

However, the recession lasted for a shorter duration than that of the previous cycle. Services trade entered the recovery phase in the years from 1992-1999.

We now turn to an examination of the performance and role of irregular shocks in services trade.

Significance of Shocks in Trade in Services

The irregular shocks (I_t) that affected total services trade are given in Figure 3.3. The shocks can be interpreted as transmission of cycles through trade integration. There were both negative and positive shocks during the study period. The regular and consistent shocks affected the sector after 1990-91.This was when there was a conscious push towards globalisation and greater trade integration through liberalisation measures. This finding supports the argument that high trade integration transmits shocks to the service sector in India.

It is important to investigate whether exports or imports are affected more by these shocks. Hence, the irregular shocks of exports and imports are derived separately, as shown in Figure 3.4. The figure indicates that shocks to services exports are higher than those to imports.

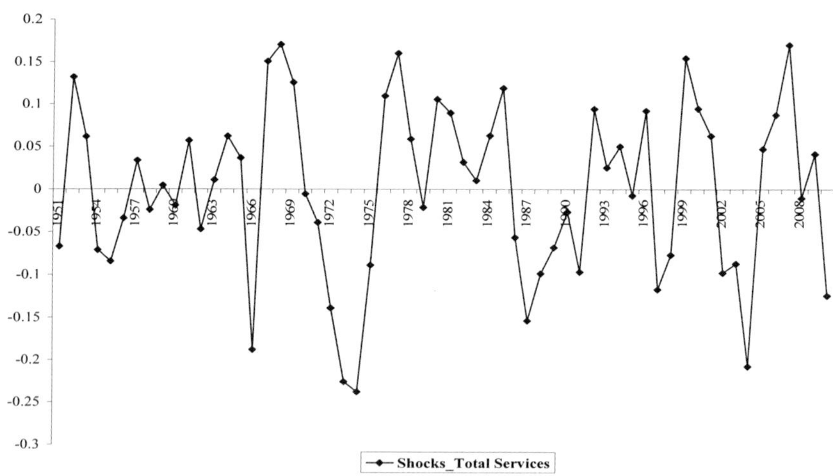

Figure 3.3: Irregular Shocks to Trade in Services (Deviation from Trend)

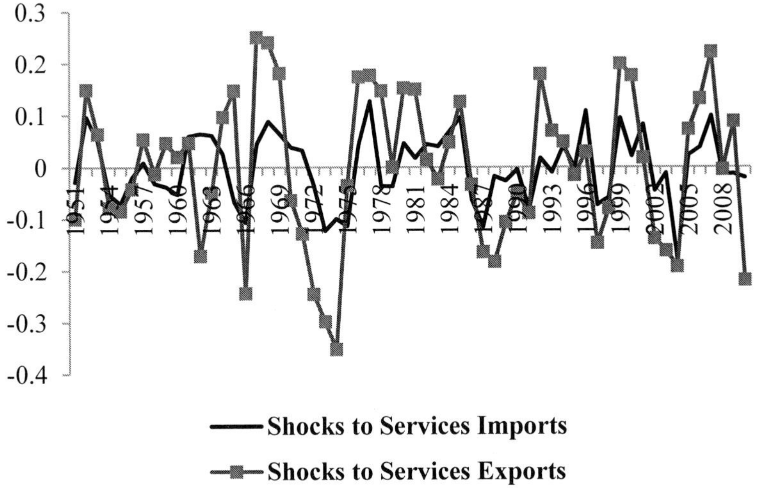

Figure 3.4: Shocks to Services Exports and Imports (Deviation from Trend)

This section identified cycles in India's trade in services from 1950-2010. It has been observed that components within trade in services played a major role in contributing to the fluctuations. Moreover, services exports are found to have been the main drivers of business cycles across countries. The shocks to services exports also exhibited a higher intensity than shocks to services imports. These findings suggest that India's export market is integrated well with the rest of the world.

Conclusions

Given that trade in services has grown over the years, the research question addressed here is whether the growth of trade in services took place gradually or whether it was a response to government policy initiatives. Did the opening up to and integration of the sector with the rest of the world pave the way for the transmission of external cyclical upturns and downturns to India?

The structural break test was used to determine the presence of breaks in services trade. Lee and Stratizicich's structural break test was used and there were no significant break years for services exports or imports. There appears to have been breaks in the GNIE component during 1988 and 1998 for services exports and 1976 and 1994 for services imports. Apart from this, in the services imports category, transport services showed significant breaks during 1964 and 1991. Further, it has also been found that structural breaks in the exports and imports of services responded differently to regime changes. The results indicate that the export trend breaks were not related to the import trend breaks. The results can be widened to imply that the growth in services trade evolved gradually over the years; it did not change abruptly, nor did it display change in response to various policy regimes initiated in the economy. The evolution might be due to the gradual integration of the Indian economy with global markets. This integration could also have widened the channel of transmission of different demand and supply shocks to the sector. These shocks in turn could generate cyclical fluctuations in international service trade flows. To analyse these cycles, the time series data was decomposed into cycles, trends and irregular shocks, and the procedure adopted by Hodrick and Prescott (1980) was applied. Three cycles were identified in the sector during the period of 1950-2010: one from 1963-64 to 1981-82; a second from 1981-82 to 1999-2000 and the third in the post-2000 period. It was observed that components or sub-sectors within trade in services played a major role in contributing to the fluctuations. Moreover, services exports appear to be more susceptible to cyclical movements across countries because shocks to exports exhibited a higher intensity than those to imports. Apparently, India's export market is integrated well with the rest of the world.

References

Balakrishnan, Pulapre and M. Parameswaran. 2007. "Understanding Economic Growth in India: A Prerequisite." *Economic and Political Weekly* 42(27-8): 2915-22.

Banga, Rashmi. 2005 "Role of Services in the Growth Process: A Survey." ICRIER Working Paper Series 159, Indian Council for Research on International Economic Relations, New Delhi.

Basu, Kaushik. 2007. "India's Dilemmas: The Political Economy of Policy-Making in a Globalized World." Paper presented at the First Sage-Madras School of Economics Endowment Lecture, Chennai, India, November 14.

Chanda, Rupa. 2009. "India." In *Trade in Services in South Asia: Opportunities and Risks of Liberalization,* edited by S.Kelegama, 23-66. Sage publications, New Delhi.

—. 2011. *Services Integration in South Asia: Trade, Investment, and Mobility*. Oxford University Press, New Delhi.

Chitre, Vikas. S. 1982. "Growth Cycles in Indian economy." *Arthvijnana*, 24(4): 293-450.

Dua, Pami and Banerji, Anirvan. 1999. "An Index of Coincident Economic Indicators for the Indian Economy." *Journal of Quantitative Economics*, 15 (2):177-201.

Dua, Pami and Banerji, Anirvan. 2007. "Predicting Indian Business Cycles: Leading Indices for External and Domestic Sectors." *The Journal of Applied Economic Research,* 1(3): 249-265.

Ghatak, Anita. 1996. "Unit Roots and Structural Breaks: The Case of India 1900-1988". *Journal of Applied Statistics*, 24 (3): 289-300.

Ghosh, Madhusudan. 1999. "Structural Break and Unit Root in Macroeconomic Time Series: Evidence from a Developing Economy." *The Indian Journal of Statistics*, 61 (2): 318-336.

GOI (Government of India). 2010-11. *Economic Survey*, New Delhi: Ministry of Finance.

Hodrick, Robert. J and Edward, C. Prescott. 1980. "Post-war U.S. Business Cycles: An Empirical Investigation." *Journal of Money, Credit and Banking* 29 (1): 1-16.

Lee, Junsoo and Mark. C. Strazicich. 2003. "Minimum Lagrange Multiplier Unit Root Test with two Structural Breaks." *Review of Economics and Statistics*, 85 (4):1082-1089.

Strazicich, Mark, C., Junsoo, Lee and Edward, Day. 2004. "Are Incomes Converging Among OECD Countries? Time Series Evidence with Two Structural Breaks." *Journal of Macroeconomics,* 26 (1): 131-145.

Mizzo, Marcela and Luc, Soete. 2001. "Internationalization of Services: A Technology Perspective." *Technological Forecasting and Social Change,* 67 (2&3): 159-185.

Mukherjee, Neela. 1983. "A Study of Invisibles and Services in India's Balance Of Payments (1950-51 to 1977-78)." *Foreign Trade Review*, 17 (4):430-441.

Panagariya, Arvind. 2008. *India the Emerging Giant.* Oxford University Press, USA.

Paul, Biru Paksha. 2010 "Liberalization and India's Business Cycle Synchronization with the U.S." *Indian Economic Review,* 45 (1):159-182.

Perron, Pierre. 1989. "The Great Crash, the Oil Price Shock, and the Unit Root Hypothesis." *Econometrica,* 57 (6): 1361-1401.

RBI (Reserve Bank of India). 1990. *Monthly Bulletin.* Mumbai. India.

—. 2010. *Monthly Bulletin.* Mumbai. India.

Appendix 3.1

Lee and Strazicich (LM) test for structural break

Lee and Strazicich (2003) proposed a model that tests endogeneity for two structural break tests. They expanded the model in line with Perron's (1989) Model C, which accounts for one structural break in the intercept and one structural break in the slope. The endogenous two break LM unit root tests proposed by Lee and Strazicich (2003) can be explained using two models: model A and model C. Both models are based on alternative assumptions about structural breaks; model A allows for two shifts in the intercept (level) and model C includes two shifts in the intercept (level) and trend. The data generating process follows:

$$y_t = \delta' Z_t + e_t , \qquad e_t = \beta e_{t-1} + \varepsilon_t \tag{1}$$

where Z_t is a vector of exogenous variables defined by the data generating process as $\left[1, t, D_{jt}\right]$ and D_{jt} is a dummy variable that denotes the time when a structural break occurs. It follows that if a break for country i occurs at T_{B_j}, then the dummy variable $D_{jt} = 1$ if $t \succ T_{B_j}$, zero and $DT_t = t - T_B$ if $t \succ T_{B_j}$. Model A allows for two shifts in level and is described by $Z = [1, t, D_{1t}, D_{2t}]$ where $D_{jt} = 1$ for $t \geq T_{B_j} + 1,\ j = 1, 2\ \&\ 0$. T_{B_j} denotes the time period when a break occurs. Model C includes two changes in level and trend and is described by $Z = [1, t, D_{1t}, D_{2t}, DT_{1t}, DT_{2t}]$, where $DT_t = t - T_B$ for $t \geq T_{B_j} + 1,\ j = 1, 2\ \&\ 0$. Note that the data generating process includes breaks under the null ($\beta = 1$) and alternative ($\beta \prec 1$) hypotheses in a consistent manner. For instance, in model A (a similar argument can be applied to model C), depending on the value of β.

Model A is specified as follows:

$$Z_t = [1, t, D_{1t}, D_{2t}] \tag{2}$$

where $D_{jt} = 1$ for $t \geq T_{B_j},\ j = 1, 2\ \&\ 0$. The break date is denoted by T_{B_j}. The null and alternative hypotheses of model A are:

$$H_0 : y_t = \mu_0 + d_1 B_{1t} + d_2 B_{2t} + y_{t-1} + v_{1t}$$
$$H_1 : y_t = \mu_1 + \gamma t + d_1 D_{1t} + d_2 D_{2t} + v_{2t}$$
(3)

The specifications of the null and alternative hypotheses of model C, respectively, are;

$$Z_t = [1, t, D_{1t}, D_{2t}, DT_{1t}, DT_{2t}]$$
(4)
$$H_0 : y_t = \mu_0 + d_1 B_{1t} + d_2 B_{2t} + d_3 D_{1t} + d_4 D_{2t} + y_{t-1} + v_{1t};$$
$$H_1 : y_t = \mu_1 + \gamma t + d_1 D_{1t} + d_2 D_{2t} + d_3 DT_{1t} + d_4 DT_{2t} + v_{2t};$$
(5)

where $DT_t = t - T_{B_j}$ for $t \geq T_{B_j}$, $j = 1,2$ & 0 ; $B_{jt} = 1$ for $t = T_{B_j} + 1$, $j = 1,2$ & 0; V_{1t} and V_{2t} denote the stationary error terms. The LM unit root test statistic can be obtained by estimating:

$$\Delta y_t = \delta \Delta Z_t + \phi \overline{S}_{t-1} + \mu_t$$
(6)

where $\overline{S} = y_t - \overline{\psi_x} - Z_t \overline{\delta}$, t=2,...T ; the regression of Δy_t provides estimates of $\overline{\delta}; \overline{\psi_x} = y_t - Z_t \overline{\delta}$ and the first observations of y_t and z_t are y_1 and z_1 respectively. The LM test statistics are provided by $\overline{\tau}$, which is the test statistic for the unit root null hypothesis that $\phi = 0$.

Since the empirical results are sensitive to lag length, we keep maximum lag length at eight years and obtain the optimal lag length on the basis of the significance of the last lag. The break dates are determined where the LM test statistic is at its minimum.

Appendix 3.2

Hodrick and Prescott (HP) Filter Method

The HP filter is a smoothing method which is used to obtain a smooth estimate of the long-term trend component of a series. It has an advantage over a simple de-trending procedure based on linear trend, which is that it is a time varying method and allows the trend to follow a stochastic process. Whereas the traditional method assumes that the trend series grows at a constant rate, the HP filter computes a smoothed series y^T of y by minimising the variance of y around y^T, subject to a penalty that constrains the second difference of y^T. The HP filter chooses y^T to minimise

$$\sum_{i=t}^{n}(y_t - y_t^T)^2 + \lambda \sum_{t=2}^{n-1}(\Delta y^T_{t+1} - \Delta y_t^T)^2 \tag{7}$$

where λ is the smoothing weight on y^T growth and n is the sample size. Hodrick and Prescott suggested the value for λ as seven for annual data. The advantages of the filter are flexibility, simplicity and reproducibility. The HP filter is employed to derive cyclical movements and irregular components or short-term shocks. Such decomposition will give a better understanding of the structural pattern.

For the present study, it is assumed that the annual series of trade in services (Y_t) has three components: trend, cyclical movements and irregular movements.

$$Y_t = T_t + C_t + I_t \tag{8}$$

where T_t= Long-run trend, C_t= Cyclical movements and I_t= Irregular movements (shocks). The HP filter is used in two stages to separate these components; first to extract the long-run trend (T_t) from the original series and then to filter out cycles (C_t) from the rest. The HP filter proceeds as follows: it assumes that a series Y_t has two components; a smooth one (T_t) and deviations of (Z_t) from T_t, that is

$$Y_t = T_t + Z_t \tag{9}$$

such that, over a long period of time, the sum of deviations (Z_t) is near zero. We apply the HP filter on Y_t to extract the trend (T_t) component from it. By subtracting T_t from the original series (Y_t) we get a new series (Z_t) that contains cyclical and irregular components.

$$Z_t = Y_t - T_t = C_t + I_t \tag{10}$$

The HP filter is again applied to Z_t. In this second stage, the HP filter splits the oscillations around the smooth component that is nothing but cycles C_t. The difference between Z_t and C_t represents shocks or irregular components (I_t).

CHAPTER FOUR

MANAGING MIGRATION AND TRADE IN SERVICES: AN OVERVIEW OF MULTILATERAL AND REGIONAL TRADE AGREEMENTS

SURABHI SINGH

Introduction

With the onset of globalization characterized by 'shrinking space, shrinking time and disappearing borders' (Human Development Report 1999), the overlap between trade and migration has also witnessed an increase, although the extent of that overlap is not very clear. For economists, migrants constitute a factor of production that is understood in terms of its economic value, and ensuring market access for these service providers is a concern. On the other hand, for migration officials, the emphasis is on border security and meeting labor market needs and on issues of social and cultural integration. The intersection of these two regimes can be perceived when the global economy requires increased market access for labor, but this increased market access for labor has to contend with regulatory barriers in industrialized countries and deal with the issues of labor market and security concerns (IOM 2013). Furthermore, when people move to provide services, it becomes trade, while the very act of movement constitutes a migration concern. To allay the fear of states regarding the repercussions of unwanted migration it is necessary that there exists a migration regime, which provides for more legal avenues for migration and ensures that the benefits accruing from the movement of workers is maintained. This chapter seeks to provide an overview of multilateral and regional trade agreements, especially in the context of Mode 4, and examine the role these agreements can play in establishing a more regulated migration regime.

By the very nature of the problem, migration is an issue where costs and benefits to countries involved in the process are inextricably linked to each other. It is an area that embodies complex linkages to issues of labor rights, labor markets, employment, trade, and national security. In this age of globalization, while barriers to the movement of goods and capital have been reduced, those on the movement of people remain intact and have even become tighter. The rules of the global economy reflect a bias towards the protection of capital over labor. Labor is a vulnerable category and migrant workers are rendered even more vulnerable by virtue of their being workers in a foreign country and in terms of their rights to not being killed and of their being given their labor rights and working standards (Hertel 2012). In the case of labor migration, the fragmentation of international law into trade and non-trade allows destination countries to pick and choose, liberalizing the trade regime for highly skilled workers under the General Agreement on Trade in Services (GATS) and concluding bilateral migration agreements for low skilled workers (Panizzon 2010).

> "The international treatment of labor migration is story (sic) of distributional and regulatory asymmetries. It responds and exacerbates rather than minimizes the historic inequality of distribution between labor and capital being increasingly (sic) replaced by the deepening wage differentials among countries—a phenomenon being fostered by free trade and economic globalization" (Panizzon 2010, 138).

It is to be noted that the International Covenant on Civil and Political Rights (ICCPR) (Article 12) establishes the right of an individual to leave a country, including his own; however, it does not establish a proportionate obligation for states to admit individuals into their own territory. Among those who migrate for work, a large number of migrants are those who are low or medium skilled and who clandestinely migrate, and these categories of migrants are also more vulnerable to abuse and exploitation.

The only multilateral agreement governing the temporary movement of workers was established by the World Trade Organization (WTO) through the General Agreement on Trade in Services (GATS). On similar lines, there have been efforts at the regional level as well, led by regional organizations. While there are 129 regional trade agreements in services that have been notified to the WTO, many of these are bilateral in nature, involving two member countries. This chapter confines itself to only those regional trade agreements that have been entered into by a regional organization. This study assumes that international organizations, as actors in their own right, create new categories of actors and form new interests for existing actors, as well as defining new international tasks that require cooperation. Besides this, the international organization as a process is always in constant evolution. International organizations act as instruments, arenas and actors in international politics (Archer 1992).

Within the category of regional trade agreements, the agreements between the European Union and its trading partners are well documented; however, relatively less attention has been paid to the progress made by other regional organizations. As a result, for the purposes of analysis, this chapter focuses on the WTO and looks upon the GATS as established by it to govern multilateral trade. Subsequently, regional trade agreements in services entered into by regional organizations, such as the North American Free Trade Agreement (NAFTA), Association of Southeast Asian Nations (ASEAN), Southern African Development Community (SADC), Caribbean Community (CARICOM), and East African Community (EAC) are examined. These regional trade agreements either have an annex on the movement of natural persons or a chapter on the movement of natural persons. This examination attempts to understand their potential to regulate migration. The chapter has been divided into four sections. The first section seeks to introduce the theme, which is carried forward in the second section that looks at trade in services and migration; it analyses the General Agreement on Trade in Services (GATS) and the provisions regarding the movement of natural persons (Mode 4). Section three looks at the progress made on the regional front by looking at some of the regional trade agreements, and is followed by concluding remarks.

Trade in Services and Migration: The Issue at Hand

Trade in services has come a long way from the time when the Uruguay round was launched and countries were uncertain about whether services were tradable as a commodity and through what medium this trade could be established. It has grown in scope and coverage over the years. World exports of commercial services amounted to USD 4170 billion in 2011 (Table 4.1).

Table 4.1: World Trade in Commercial Services by Category, 2011

(Billion dollars and percentage)

	Value	Share				
	2011	2000	2005	2009	2010	2011
Exports						
All commercial services	4170	100.0	100.0	100.0	100.0	100.0
Transportation services	860	23.0	22.7	20.0	21.0	20.6
Travel	1065	32.1	27.7	25.5	25.2	25.6
Other commercial services	2240	44.8	49.6	54.4	53.7	53.7
Imports						
All commercial services	3955	100.0	100.0	100.0	100.0	100.0
Transportation services	1100	28.7	28.8	25.4	27.3	27.9
Travel	950	29.9	27.0	24.4	24.1	24.0
Other commercial services	1860	41.4	44.2	48.9	47.5	47.1

Note: Total commercial services do not add up to the sum of componen:s because of unallocated services, accounting for 0.3 per cent of world exports and 0.6 per cent of world imports in 2011. For more information on asymmetries, see the Metadata.

Source: WTO Secretariat

Today, services can be traded through various media and one medium, which is of importance for the purpose of this chapter, is services supplied through the temporary movement of natural persons, or Mode 4, as provided for in the General Agreement on Trade in Services. It is in the category of temporary movement of natural persons that this chapter seeks to situate migrating for work, as the GATS agreement declares that it pertains to trade but not labor related matters.[10] Martin (2006) argues that it is an unsustainable argument that GATS applies to service providers but not migrant workers. Using the example of the US H1-B programme, he illustrates how temporary migrant workers who are service providers end up settling in the US. An analysis of the international framework governing the movement of migrant workers is outside the scope of this chapter, but some general observations need to be kept in mind before the detailed analysis of GATS that follows.

The commitments of Mode 4 are usually horizontal in nature and this pattern is true for both developed and developing countries.[11] The analysis of Mode 4 that follows is essentially horizontal in nature, as the objective of the chapter is not to delve into sector-specific commitments of member countries. The attempt here is to evaluate how Mode 4 as a regulatory framework is associated with the phenomenon of migrating for work, rather than probe the level of sector-specific commitments related to Mode 4. Furthermore, even though GATS does not mention skill level, the commitments of member countries have maintained a bias towards the highly skilled. Most Mode 4 commitments have sought to liberalize the movement of business people and intra-corporate transferees, who are highly skilled professionals, and very often this movement is tied with Mode 3, i.e. commercial presence. 60 per cent of GATS schedules with horizontal Mode 4 commitments include intra-corporate transferees (ICTs).

Mode 4 seeks to facilitate the movement of workers but does not specify how this movement is to be managed. Member states of the WTO have retained the right to formulate and implement the policies they

[10] The Singapore Declaration, 1996, laid out that ILO was a competent agency for dealing with labor issues and that the WTO would continue its informal cooperation with the ILO.

[11] The lack of sector-specific commitments is reflective of the 'homogenous nature of immigration regimes across service sectors in most countries' (Carzaniga 2008, 481). These horizontal commitments are also subject to many restrictions, such as the duration of stay, labor market and economic needs test, entry restriction for certain sectors and so on (Chanda 2002). There has been a dearth of commitments that address the need of sectors where the movement of service suppliers is crucial to the supply of a service, such as in construction related services or health services.

choose (Nonnenmacher 2012). In practice, the bound levels of commitments of member countries are often below the actual levels of liberalization prevalent in those countries. A detailed look at GATS should shed more light on the issues raised.

General Agreement on Trade in Services and Mode 4

The liberalization of the movement of individuals - in GATS parlance "natural persons" - has recently been brought into trade negotiations in the Uruguay Round of Negotiations (1986-1994) (Nonnemacher 2012). During the General Agreement on Tariffs and Trade (GATT) years, not much attention was paid to the issue of services in general and movement of people in particular. In the 1982 GATT ministerial meeting, an attempt was made by the US to put services on the agenda, which led to the establishment of a GATT work program on services, as a result of which, major countries, although resistant to the idea of the inclusion of services, nevertheless agreed to undertake national studies of their service sectors (Hoekman and Kostecski 2009); as a result, trade in services was subsequently included in the Uruguay Round. This inclusion of services culminated in the General Agreement of Trade in Services and it became an inalienable part of the World Trade Organization. It was rendered necessary because services trade is different from goods trade, being intangible in nature, and often the provision of supply of a service requires that a service supplier and receiver are present simultaneously.[12]

How does the GATS relate to labor mobility? Two of the four modes of the General Agreement on Trade in Services have human mobility implications – Mode 2 (consumption abroad) and Mode 4 (Movement of Natural Persons to Supply Service). The GATS conceives of labor as an internationally tradable service, and Mode 4 as one of the media of supplying service, specifically involving the movement of labor for the

---

[12] There are 11 service sectors identified by the WTO for trade in services and in each of these service sectors, services can be provided through four modes/media. Mode 1 refers to cross-border supply where the service can be provided from the territory of one member country to another without the physical movement of the service supplier, such as advisory services. Mode 2 refers to consumption abroad, whereby the consumer of a particular service physically moves from one country to another, such as in the case of tourism service. Mode 3 refers to commercial presence, where the service supplier establishes a legal territorial presence in another country to provide the services. An instance of Mode 3 service would be a foreign bank establishing a subsidiary in India. Mode 4 refers to the temporary movement of natural persons to provide services.

purpose of supplying a service in another country (Carzaniga 2003 in Broude 2007). Mode 4 related movements can take place in any of the sectors pursuant to horizontal or vertical commitments that a member country agrees to undertake, but certain sectors, like health services, construction services and tourism services, are more prone to the movement of labor to supply services. It is to be noted that while GATS applies to service related labor migration, it does not establish free movement of unemployed labor (Broude 2007).

Further details on the coverage of GATS are provided in the *Annex on the Movement of Natural Persons Supplying Services under the Agreement.* The Annex specifies that GATS does not apply to natural persons seeking employment in a foreign market, nor does it apply to measures 'regarding citizenship, residence or employment on a permanent basis'. It is this caveat in the Annex that separates GATS commitments from immigration laws, and service providers from labor (Broude 2007). It translates into the fact that those who enter a foreign market do so as service providers. These individuals cannot seek access to foreign markets as employment seekers.

However, Mode 4 affects the politics of migrating for work, because it involves the movement of *people* across borders, and this movement has social implications that are not present or are less relevant than in goods and capital trade.[13] It makes people who migrate very different from other factors of production. It has been widely argued in the literature that WTO should acknowledge the human rights implications of its work and contribute to better living conditions, reflecting the needs of all member

[13] There has been a raging debate on promoting labor rights as human rights and including labor standards within the WTO structure to promote their effective implementation. Labor rights activists argue that there is a need for universally accepted human rights regarding working conditions that would be applicable across all nations (Brown 2001). A possible means to ensure this is to link labor standards with the WTO so that the competitiveness of countries based on low wages and weak labor laws is done away with. The opponents of this argument postulate that it is a veiled form of protectionism. They argue that developed countries would benefit from stringent labor laws in developing countries, as it would offset the cost of having higher labor standards in their own countries; hence, the competitiveness of developing countries based on abundant supply of labor should be retained. Labor laws fall within domestic jurisdictions and hence, cannot be included in international trade negotiations (Brown 2001). In the context of WTO, in the 1996 Singapore Ministerial Declaration, it was laid out that while all member countries agree to internationally recognized core labor standards and affirm their support of the promotion of these standards, it was the ILO that was the competent body for dealing with and promoting these standards.

countries (Zagel 2005; Robinson 2001). As Normand (2000) has argued, trade law has superseded human rights law to the extent that violation of human rights is being carried out in the name of international trade. While the prevalent view has been that the human rights provisions have the effect of restricting trade, Panizzon (2006) puts forward the view that only human rights compliant trade has the potential to benefit everyone.

Panizzon (2006) argues that human rights are more closely related to trade in services, because in Mode 4, a human being is the object of physical movement across a border. GATS currently covers the most privileged of migrant workers, who face fewer human right risks, and although it does not define the skill level of the services to which Mode 4 applies, hardly any states have made commitments for low skilled workers. Most of the Mode 4 commitments being horizontal in nature, members have scheduled an initial ‘Unbound’ (no commitments) and then qualified it by granting access to select categories of persons (Winters 2005). Even the limited commitments that have been made are biased towards persons linked to a commercial presence and highly skilled persons (Chanda 1999). Only a few schedules guarantee commitments under Mode 4 that are not linked to commercial presence (Carzaniga 2008; Winters 2005). Furthermore, the liberalisation has taken place does not provide for unconditional access but rather is subject to market access and national treatment regulations.

Most countries that allow for the entry of the self-employed require migrant workers to deliver services to the final consumer, rendering it extremely tenuous, for few developing country service providers have the contacts to find consumers abroad (Martin 2005). Developing countries are seeking liberalization in favor of less skilled service providers, as it is this group that they wish to send abroad for work, as they are a large group numerically when compared to intra-corporate transferees. However, even in developing countries, the impact of the exit of service providers is unclear, making developing countries cautious in seeking more relaxation of Mode 4. Further, any request for liberalization would also involve concessions on the part of the developing countries.

Suave (2008) argues that developing countries have hope for Mode 4 liberalization in the form of the Doha Development Agenda, but it is necessary to keep rational expectations. There are three main challenges that make Mode 4 liberalization difficult. First, there is reluctance on the part of labor market and immigration officials in receiving countries to accept semi-permanent legal commitments in a trade setting such as the WTO. As a matter of precaution, commitments are scheduled at a lower level than the actual requirement for temporary labor. Second, the most favored nation status that members are obliged to bestow under the GATS is a privilege that most member countries are reluctant to offer. On the contrary, bilateral guest worker programs and labor cooperation agreements continue to hold importance. Third, there is an inherent bias in trade negotiations towards those who are highly skilled, and much of the movement in this category is pursuant to Mode 3, which favors the capital exporting countries. There has been considerable emphasis by developing countries on delinking Mode 4 from Mode 3 under the Doha Development Agenda, but given these complications, progress on Mode 4 negotiations continues to be slow (Suave 2008).

It has been argued that GATS can provide an avenue for legal migration by offering predictable opportunities for lower skilled workers, and thus could reduce illegal migration and the accompanying human rights violations (Donmen 2005). From a human rights perspective, Mode 4 can also have important implications, as by addressing temporary migration, it allows migrant workers to work abroad where jobs are available. Although GATS does not define the term 'temporary' when referring to Mode 4, it ranges from a few weeks to three years, based on the manner in which WTO members have liberalised temporary movement pursuant to Mode 4. Hence a commitment by a country "A" liberalizing the movement of temporary workers for a few weeks falls under the rubric of Mode 4 and so does a commitment by country "B" liberalizing movement for three years. The international dimensions of human rights are receiving more and more attention today. The Committee on Economic Social and Cultural Rights, for instance, has often expressed concern about the way countries' international trade-related obligations affect human rights (Donmen 2005). However, lack of understanding on the part of trade policy makers and the reluctance to take cognizance of the migration aspects of Mode 4 movement have resulted in a stalemate over Mode 4 negotiations.[14] The next section turns to the regional front and looks at the progress achieved by regional trade agreements and the prospects they offer in managing migration.

---

[14] Multilateral agreements work on the principle of guaranteed access to foreign markets for all the parties involved, while economic migration policy is about regulating the entry of labor into other countries' markets, depending on the economic situation of the countries and taking cognizance of the political and cultural issues involved (Nonnamacher 2012).

Regional Trade Agreements[15]

In recent years, when negotiations on the multilateral front do not seem to be making much progress, many regional trade agreements (RTAs) have come into force, providing preferential treatment to the parties concerned. RTAs are reciprocal trade agreements between two or more partners. RTAs are considered beneficial because it is held that successful liberalization among neighbouring states will pave the way for subsequent multilateral liberalization (Bhagwati 1993). By July 31st, 2013, about 575 agreements had been reported to the WTO, of which 379 were in force (inclusive of both goods and services) (WTO 2013).

Most member countries of the WTO are members of at least one regional trade agreement. The surge in the number of regional agreements can be attributed to the deadlock in negotiations in the Doha Development Round, the conclusion of many comprehensive preferential trade agreements (PTAs) by the European Union (EU) and US and the perceived need to achieve deeper integration through liberalization of investment, labor and other new areas required to support production networks (Chanda 2011). RTAs can be between neighboring countries such as South-South (ASEAN-China), free trade agreements (FTAs) or North-North FTAs (US-Korea), or can be cross-regional in nature, such North-South FTAs (Japan-Philippines). They can include varying combinations of partners who differ in their income levels, or exist between a group of countries or a regional grouping and a country.

Although there are a vast number of regional trade agreements in operation that cover both goods and services, this chapter looks at regional agreements on services that have been entered into by regional organizations such as the North American Free Trade Association (NAFTA), Association of Southeast Asian Nations (ASEAN), Southern African Development Community (SADC), Andean Community, Caribbean Community (CARICOM) and East African Community

---

[15] As far as trade in services is concerned, the provisions for regional trade arrangements are laid out in Article V of GATS. "This Agreement shall not prevent any of its Members from being a party to or entering into an agreement liberalizing trade in services between or among the parties to such an agreement, provided that such an agreement (a) has substantial sectoral coverage, and (b) provides for the absence or elimination of substantially all discrimination, in the sense of Article XVII, between or among the parties, in the sectors covered under subparagraph" (Para 1 of Article V, GATS).

(EAC).[16] This chapter has sought to confine itself to trade agreements entered into by international and regional organizations as it is based on the premise that international organizations are actors in their own rights, with significant power to shape interests for new as well as existing actors, as outlined in the foregoing sections. Furthermore, there has been a relative dearth of work on these regional trade agreements when compared to the abundance of studies examining trade agreements entered into by the European Union (EU) and its partner countries. The attempt here is not to delve into the debate over whether regionalism is a better option than multilateralism, but to look at regional commitments concerning trade in services and the provisions they have regarding movement of natural persons and analyse whether they can contribute towards an orderly migration regime. The emphasis is on the conceptual framework of the agreements and the scope they offer. The focus of the section is not on trade benefits accruing from these agreements, but how they can contribute towards migration management. Another point to be emphasized is that the analysis of the RTAs is essentially horizontal, meaning they apply to all the sectors under consideration, which is similar to the approach used to look at GATS commitments. The focal point of analysis is the categories of persons covered in RTAs and the conditions of access applicable to them.

North American Free Trade Agreement (NAFTA)

The NAFTA, between the United States, Canada and Mexico, that came into force on January 1st, 1994, predates the GATS. It has a separate chapter (Chapter 12) on cross-border trade in services and another on temporary entry for business persons (Chapter 16). The provisions in the chapter on cross-border trade in services are symmetric to GATS obligations and, like the GATS, it provides no obligations for the concerned parties to provide access to employment to nationals of member countries. However, it lays down detailed criteria for the grant and refusal of temporary entry. The immigration aspects related to temporary entry are also given due recognition. For instance, Paragraph 1 of Annex 1603 (Chapter 16) states:

---

[16] Agreements between the EU and its trading partners have not been included in the analysis as the level of integration achieved by the European Union has not been attained by any other regional grouping. Besides, while the European experience has been fairly well documented, the experiences of the South have not received so much attention.

> "Each Party shall grant temporary entry to a business person seeking to engage in a business activity set out in Appendix 1603.A.1, without requiring that person to obtain an employment authorization, provided that the business person otherwise complies with existing immigration measures applicable to temporary entry."

It allows for the temporary entry of business visitors, traders and investors, intra-corporate transferees and professionals (a detailed list of which is given in Appendix 1603 D.1 of the NAFTA along with the educational requirement for each).

Association of Southeast Asian Nations (ASEAN)

ASEAN has adopted the World Trade Organization's GATS terminology for its regional trade negotiations. Following the pattern of GATS commitments, under the ASEAN Framework Agreement on Services (AFAS), six ASEAN countries (Singapore, Brunei Darussalam, Malaysia, Thailand, the Philippines and Indonesia) have restricted their commitments on foreign service providers to skilled occupations such as specialists and senior managerial personnel, and access to the labor market is restricted under AFAS (Bhatnagar and Manning 2005). Besides AFAS, ASEAN has also entered into a regional trade agreement with Australia and New Zealand. The ASEAN-Australia-New Zealand Free Trade Agreement, which came in force in January 2010, has a separate chapter on the movement of natural persons and an annex on schedules of movement of natural persons. It provides for rights and obligations additional to those set out in the trade in services agreement. It also acknowledges the need to establish transparent and streamlined procedures for completing immigration formalities. It includes installers and service suppliers as well as contractual service suppliers. It requires each party to provide for a schedule containing its commitment on temporary entry in its annex. It also has transparency requirements requiring the parties to publish relevant immigration formalities.

Bhatnagar and Manning, in their 2005 study, looked at the ASEAN Framework Agreement on Services (AFAS), which, until 2000, was the only agreement on trade in services in Asia, and came to the conclusion that the main aim of trade agreements that have migration clauses is to promote trade, and addressing the migration issue is a peripheral goal. Furthermore, they also argue, based on the commitments under AFAS made by the parties concerned, that regional trade agreements do not differ from multilateral negotiations when it comes to regulating the entry of foreign service providers.

Southern African Development Community (SADC)

SADC has a protocol on trade in services that seeks to achieve liberalization in such a way that “each member will treat services emanating from other members and the supplier of such services, in the same way as its own services suppliers and the services they supply” (SADC Protocol on Trade in Services). The protocol is not applicable to natural persons seeking or taking employment in the labor market of a state party, nor does it confer access to the labor market of another state party. SADC has put in place a draft protocol on the movement of natural persons called the Protocol on the Facilitation of the Movement of Persons. The draft protocol has not yet come into force, but its eventual aim is to eliminate obstacles to the movement of persons of the region within the territories of the state parties concerned. It envisions a region where citizens enjoy visa free entry, residence, and establishment in the territories of member states. Visa free entry is allowed for visitors but not to those entering for employment purposes. Whether residence permits entail the possibility of being able to work depends on domestic law and the classification of residence permits.

Caribbean Community (CARICOM)

In the Caribbean region, a provision regarding the free movement of temporary service providers can be found in the Revised Treaty of Chaguaramas (2001). The preamble to the treaty specifies that members of the region are:

> “**Aware** that optimal production by economic enterprises in the Community requires the structured integration of production in the Region, and particularly, the unrestricted movement of capital, labour and technology; **Resolved** to establish conditions which would facilitate access by their nationals to the collective resources of the Region on a non-discriminatory basis.”

Chapter Three of the treaty speaks of the establishment of services, capital and the movement of community nationals. Article 46 of the treaty provides university graduates, media workers, sportspersons, artists and musicians the right to seek employment, depending on the recognition of their qualification by the relevant authorities of the receiving member states. To facilitate the movement of community nationals, the treaty seeks to streamline visa processes, and there is recognition of administrative requirements such as the recognition of qualifications to provide for accrediting institutions and the harmonisation of social security benefits.

East African Community (EAC) and Other Initiatives

In Africa, The East African Community has an annex on the movement of workers, in addition to their schedule on trade in services. The Annex on the Movement of Workers lays down detailed conditions for getting work permits for employment in the territory of another member state. To prevent risk to and the abuse of foreign workers, there are detailed guidelines about cancellation of work permits, employment of spouses and children, expulsion and deportation and employment. For instance, Regulation 7 (denial or work permit) of the Annex on the Movement of Workers posits that the grounds for the cancellation of a work permit shall be made known to the worker, and the worker must be given enough time to leave the country; Regulation 9 (employment of spouse and child) allows for the employment of the spouse or child of the worker in the worker's host partner state in accordance with the national laws of the partner state; Regulation 12 (access to employment opportunities) states that the partner state shall endeavor to collect and disseminate information on job vacancies to assist the citizens of partner states with respect to job opportunities, and Regulation 13 (equal treatment in employment) stipulates equal treatment in employment to citizens of partners states of the community.

There have been regional initiatives such as the Asia Pacific Economic Co-operation (APEC) business card initiative to foster mobility of business persons. Further, Decision 439 of the Andean Community establishes a "general framework of principles and rules for liberalizing the trade in services in the Andean Community". Within the framework agreed to by the Andean Council of Ministers of Foreign Affairs, the decision envisages facilitating the free movement and temporary presence of natural or physical persons. Echoing similarities with other agreements, it speaks of recognition of licences, certifications, professional degrees and other such documents.

Regional arrangements differ across the world in the objectives they try to achieve, so the provisions in one regional agreement cannot be compared to those in another similar agreement. However, some observations can be made at a broad level. Multilateral negotiations have not been able to make substantial progress as far as Mode 4 is concerned, although there have been proposals from countries like India, Argentina, Chile and other countries with similar demands, which stress the importance of using standard terminology for the scheduling of commitments and the need for eliminating discriminatory practices, mutual recognition of qualifications and streamlining immigration procedures. However, some progress has been achieved on the regional front. There is recognition of the link between immigration issues and trade in services, as manifested in the draft SADC protocol on the movement of natural persons, which seeks to eliminate barriers to the free movement of natural persons. Based on an analysis of the AFAS, Bhatnagar and Manning (2005) conclude that RTAs have to contend with political opposition to become an alternative to the liberalization of Mode 4, but it is smaller groupings like the East African Community that have linked the movement of workers to trade in services and established detailed guidelines to foster the movement of workers within regions while simultaneously linking it with the migration question.

Conclusion

This chapter sought to look at multilateral and regional trade agreements and the framework they provide for governing the movement of service providers in the context of Mode 4. GATS is the only multilateral framework that seeks to liberalize the movement of natural persons and it also promotes temporary and circulatory migration, but its main problem lies in ensuring temporariness (UNCTAD 2010). Barriers are embedded in national immigration laws, which are more difficult to regulate than a reduction in tariff levels. Besides, the scope of Mode 4 is difficult to identify because of the problem of determining what constitutes a service. While GATS does not apply to migration for employment or to permanent migration, and covers only temporary mobility in respect to the supply of a service, there is a labor dimension attached. The movement of migrant workers, although termed differently in GATS, is actually trans-border labor movement. Trade and labor are often viewed as binaries, but it is overlooked that any traded good or service involves input in the form of human labor. There is a need to look at Mode 4 in its own right and deal with associated migration issues.

Developing countries have a comparative advantage in labor, especially in sectors such as agriculture and labor intensive manufacturing sectors, and have complained that developed countries have limited the scope of negotiations on international migration to the services sector. There has been exclusion of groups in the agriculture and manufacturing sectors in services negotiations and it is the working populations of these sectors that form the abundance of labor supply in developing countries.

From the perspective of developed countries, liberalizing low skilled occupations is a politically challenging task. The bias in Mode 4 towards those who are highly skilled leaves out medium skilled workers such as nurses, technicians, and data entry operators. The important question that needs attention is how to integrate these movements of temporary workers in the international trading system in a more predictable manner and help establish a more predictable regime for migrating for work.

As compared to GATS, regional trade agreements serve these needs better. NAFTA is one of the earliest agreements with a specific chapter on the temporary movement of natural persons. Furthermore, the NAFTA agreement also takes cognizance of the links between border security, domestic labor and the employment scenarios of member countries. It has been argued that, as fewer countries are involved at the regional level compared to a multilateral setting like the WTO, it is relatively easy to achieve trade liberalization at the regional level, which is fostered by shared history and cultural and linguistic affinities. The stalemate over multilateral negotiations indicates that countries are unwilling to grant the most favored nation (MFN) status pursuant to their Mode 4 commitments in WTO, preferring regional arrangements to facilitate the temporary entry of service providers. In addition, there is an evolving understanding at the regional level of the interconnections between trade and migration issues, as reflected, for instance, in the initiatives taken by the East African Community (EAC) and Caribbean Community (CARICOM).

Migration and trade policies are not integrated today to factor in the overlapping concerns of each, and are often negotiated by government ministries with their own set of agendas. However, trade, immigration, labor market and social policies cannot be viewed as isolated from each other, so there is an urgent need to integrate immigration and labor market perspectives with trade policy issues. The main barriers to Mode 4 are immigration policy and social security issues, inadequate recognition of qualifications and discriminatory treatment of foreign service providers, which are also the concerns of migration policy planners. The GATS is not a migration agreement and neither are other regional trade agreements; their primary goal is to achieve trade liberalization, and migration is just an ancillary goal. However, it needs to be stressed that the primary aim behind trade is to foster development. Undeniably, it was one of the primary goals behind the establishment of WTO – to foster development through trade liberalization. The current scenario of trade liberalization operates to promote the movement of the highly skilled (albeit in a limited way), to the neglect of the medium and low skilled. By leaving out these groups, it is working against the very motive that led to its establishment.

The inclusion of these groups within the realm of trade agreements would provide a predictable means of migrating for work and, by virtue of being temporary in nature, would preclude the possibility of their affecting the economies of the host countries. Regional agreements seem to offer the prospect of linking migration with trade and, given the logjam witnessed in WTO ministerial conferences, are fast emerging as a more viable alternative.

References

Asean-Australia-New Zealand Free Trade Agreement. 2012. "Agreement Establishing The Asean-Australia-New Zealand Free Trade Area." Accessed July 12. http://www.asean.fta.govt.nz/assets/Agreement-Establishing-the-ASEAN-Australia-New-Zealand-Free-Trade-Area.pdf.

Archer, Clive. 1992. *International Organizations*, London and New York: Routledge.

Bhagwati, J. 1993. "Regionalism and Multilateralism: An Overview", in *New Dimensions in Regional Integration,* edited by A. Panagariya and J. de Melo .Washington DC: World Bank.

Bhatnagar, P. and C Manning. 2005. "Regional arrangements for mode 4 in the services sector: lesson from the ASEAN experience?" *World Trade Review* 4(2):171-199.

Broude, Tomer. 2007. "Moral Aspects of International Labour Migration Regimes." *Proceedings of the Annual Meeting (American Society of International Law)* 101 (March 28-31): 313-318.

Brown, Drussila K. 2001. "Labour Standards: Where Do They Belong on the International Trade Agenda?" *The Journal of Economic Perspectives*.15 (3):89-112.

Carazaniga, Antonia. 2003. "The GATS, Mode 4, and Pattern of Commitments." in *Moving People to Deliver Services* edited by Aaditya Mattoo and Antonia Carzaniga, Washington DC: World Bank.

—. 2008. "A warmer welcome? Access for Natural Persons under PTAs". In *Opening Markets for Trade in Services: Countries and Sectors in Bilateral and WTO Negotiations*, edited by Juan A. Marchetti and Martin Roy, Cambridge: Cambridge University Press.

Chanda, Rupa. 1999. "Movement of Natural Persons and Trade in Services: Liberalising Temporary Movement of Labour under GATS." Working Paper No. 51, Indian Council for Research on International Economic Relations.

—. 2002. "Movement of Natural Persons and The GATS: Major Policy Impediments." in *Development, Trade and the WTO: A Handbook,* edited by Bernard Hoekman and Aaditya Mattoo. Washington DC: World Bank.

—. "Mapping the Universe of Services Disciplines in Asian PTAs." NCCR Trade Working Paper, No 2011/May 2011, http://www.wti.org/fileadmin/user_upload/nccrtrade.ch/wp2/people/WPed5ed%20Mapping%20the%20Universe%20of%20Services%20Disciplines%20in%20Asian%20PTAs%20_2_reply%20may.pdf. Accessed on May 30, 2013).

Donmen, Caroline. 2005. "Migrants' Human Rights: Could GATS Help?" *Migration Information Source*. Accessed on February 2, 2013. http://www.migrationinformation.org/feature/display.cfm?id=290.

Ghosh, Bimal. 2007. "Managing Migration: Wither the Missing Regime? How Relevant is Trade Law to Such a Regime." *Proceedings of the Annual Meeting (American Society of International Law)* 101 (March 28-31, 2007): 303-306.

Hertel, Shareen. 2012. "Human Rights and the Global Economy: Bringing Labour Rights Back In." Accessed on February 12, 2013. http://www.law.umaryland.edu/academics/journals/mjil/documents/vol_24_21.pdf.

Hoekman, M Bernard and Michel M. Kostecki 1995. *The Political Economy of the World Trading System - The WTO and Beyond*, New York: Oxford University Press reprinted 2009.

"Human Development Report" (HDR) 1999. New York: Oxford University Press.

International Organization for Migration (IOM) 2013. "Migration and Trade." *International Organization for Migration*. Accessed on August 5, 2013. http://www.rcmvs.org/documentos/IOM_EMM/v2/V2S04_CM.pdf.

Martin, Philip. 2005. "*Migrants in the Global Labor Market.*" Accessed on March 15, 2011. http:// www.gcim.org/attachements/TP1.pdf.

—. 2006. "GATS, Migration, and Labour Standards". Discussion Paper, Geneva: International Institute of Labour Studies.

North American Free Trade Agreement. Accessed on September 15, 2012. https://www.nafta-sec-alena.org/Default.aspx?tabid=97&language=en-US.

Normand, Roger. 2000. "Separate and Unequal: Trade and Human Rights Regimes." Background Paper for HDR 2000. Accessed on February 1, 2013. http://hdr.undp.org/en/reports/global/hdr2000/papers/normand2000.pdf.

Nonnenmacher, Sophie. 2012. " International Trade Law and Labour Mobility" in *Foundations of International Migration Law*, edited by Brian Opeskin, Richard Perruchoud, Jilyanne Redpath-Cross. Cambridge: Cambridge University Press.

Panizzon, Marion. 2006. "How close would GATS Get to Human Rights?", Working Paper No 2006/14. Accessed on March 15, 2013. http://papers.ssrn.com/sol3/papers.cfm?abstract_id=1090862.

—. "Temporary Movement of Workers and Human Rights Protection: Interfacing the "Mode 4" of GATS with Non-Trade Bilateral Migration Agreements." *Proceedings of the Annual Meeting (American Society of International Law),* no.104 (March 24-27, 2010), 2010: 131-139.

Revised Treaty of Chaguaramas Establishing the Caribbean Community including the Caricom Single Market and Economy. Accessed on July 5, 2013. http://www.sice.oas.org/trade/caricom/caricind.asp.

Robinson, Mary. 2001. "Making the Global Economy Work for Human Rights." in *The Role of the World Trade Organization in Global Governance*, edited by Gary P Sampson. United Nations University Press.

SADC Protocol on Trade in Services. Accessed on August 1, 2013. http://www.sadc.int/files/7313/6439/6118/Protocol_on_Trade_in_Services_-_2012_-_English.pdf.

Suave Pierre. 2008. "Been there, not yet done that: Lessons and challenges in Services trade." in *GATS and the Regulation of International Trade in Services*, edited by Marion Panizzon, Nicole Pohl and Pierre Suave ed. New York: Cambridge University Press.

The East African Community Common Market (Free Movement of Workers) Regulations. Accessed on July 30, 2013. http://www.eac.int/commonmarket/documentation/doc_download/46-annex-on-the-free-movement-of-workers.html.

United Nations Conference on Trade and Development (UNCTAD). 2010. "Towards SADC Liberalisation: Balancing Multiple Imperatives." Geneva: UNCTAD.

Winters, L. Alan. 2005 "Developing Country Proposals for the Liberalisation of Movements of Natural Service Suppliers." In *Reforming the World Trading System: Legitimacy, Efficiency and Democratic Governance,* edited by in Ernst-Ulrich-Petersmann. New York: Oxford University Press.

WTO Secretariat. "Trade in Services data". 2013. Accessed on August 2, 2013. http://www.wto.org/english/res_e/statis_e/its2012_e/its12_trade_category_e.htm

WTO. "Regional Trade Agreements." 2013. Accessed on July 25, 2013. http://www.wto.org/english/tratop_e/region_e/region_e.htm.

Zagel, Gudrun Monika. 2005. "WTO and Human Rights: Examining Linkages and Suggesting Convergence", *International Development Law Organization- Jurist Paper Series*. 2(2)

CHAPTER FIVE

AN ANALYSIS OF PATTERNS AND TRENDS IN FDI AND ITS IMPACT ON INDIA'S SERVICES SECTOR DURING THE PRE- AND POST-GLOBAL CRISIS PERIOD

ADITI SAWANT

Introduction

India's services sector expanded rapidly, with double-digit growth, in the 2000s. As the Euro crisis has worsened, growth has slowed, although the sector is still growing at a much higher rate compared to other sectors of the economy (Government of India 2013, 1).

Despite having immense natural resources such as fertile land, an abundance of water, minerals and competent human resources, the agriculture and industrial sectors have been woefully neglected in India. The new growth driver has been the services sector, propelled by the liberalisation policies of the Government of India since 1991. FDI policies between 1991 and 2011 have been focused more on services than the manufacturing and agriculture sectors.

Services in India

The services sector covers a wide array of activities and includes the most sophisticated sectors, like telecommunications, satellite mapping and computer software, simple services such as those performed by the barber, the carpenter and the plumber, highly capital-intensive activities like civil aviation and shipping, employment-oriented activities like tourism, real estate and housing, infrastructure-related activities like railways and ports, and social sector-related activities like health and education.

The national accounts classification of the services sector incorporates trade, hotels, and restaurants; transport, storage and communication; financing, insurance, real estate and business services, and community, social and personal services. In the World Trade Organization (WTO) list of services and the Reserve Bank of India' (RBI) classification, construction is also included.

India's services sector has emerged as a prominent sector in terms of its contribution to national and state incomes, trade flows, FDI flows and employment. The share of services in India's GDP at factor cost (at current prices) increased from 33.3 per cent in 1950-51 to 56.5 per cent in 2012-13. If construction is included, the share increases to 64.8 per cent in 2012-13. With an 18.0 per cent share of trade, hotels and restaurants as a group is the largest contributor to GDP among the various services sub-sectors, followed by financing, insurance, real estate and business services with a 16.6 per cent share. Both these service groups have shown perceptible improvement in their shares over the years. Community, social and personal services, with a share of 14.0 per cent, is in third place. Construction, a borderline services inclusion, is in fourth place with an 8.2 per cent share (Government of India 2013, 213).

Table 5.1: Rate of Growth of Services Sector GDP at Factor Cost at 2004-2005 Prices (in per cent)

Service Sector	2005-06	2006-07	2007-08	2008-09	2009-10	2010-11	2011-12	2012-13
Construction	12.80	10.30	10.80	5.30	6.70	10.20	5.60	5.90
Trade, Hotels, Transport and Communication	12.00	11.60	10.90	7.50	10.40	12.30	7.00	5.20
Financing, Insurance, Real Estate and Business Services	12.60	14.00	12.00	12.00	9.70	10.10	11.70	8.60
Community, Social and Personal Services	7.10	2.80	6.90	12.50	11.70	4.30	6.00	6.80

Source: RBI, Statistical Handbook of Indian Economy, 2012-13

FDI in Services Sector in India

The growth of the services sector is closely linked to the FDI inflows into this sector and the role of transnational firms. While the ambiguity in classifying different activities under the services sector continues, the combined FDI share of financial and non-financial services, construction development, telecommunications, computer hardware and software, and hotels and tourism can be taken as a rough estimate of the FDI share in services, although it may include some non-service elements. This share was 47 per cent of the cumulative FDI equity inflows during the period of April 2000-November 2012. The five service sectors are also the sectors attracting the highest cumulative FDI inflows to the economy, with financial and non-financial services topping the list at USD 36.04 billion during the period of April 2000-November 2012. This is followed by other service sectors – construction development (USD 21.77 billion), telecommunication (USD 12.62 billion), and computer software and hardware (USD 11.54 billion). If the shares of some other services or service-related sectors, like trading (1.96 per cent), information and broadcasting (1.65 per cent), consultancy services (1.11 per cent), construction (infrastructure) activities (1.06), ports (0.88 per cent), agriculture services (0.80 per cent), hospital and diagnostic centres (0.82 per cent), education (0.36 per cent), air transport including air freight (0.24 per cent), and retail trading (0.02 per cent) are included, the total share of cumulative FDI inflows to the services sector becomes 56.08 per cent (Government of India 2013, 215).

In 2011-12, FDI inflows to the services sector (top five sectors including construction) grew robustly, by 57.62 per cent, to USD 12.14 billion, compared to the growth of total FDI inflows at 33.6 per cent. However, in 2012-13 (April-November), overall FDI inflows fell by 43.3 per cent, to USD 15.85 billion from USD 27.93 billion in the corresponding period of the previous year. Following this trend, FDI inflows to the top five services also fell by 9.7 per cent, to USD 8.19 billion. While FDI inflows to the top four services sectors fell by amounts in the range of 14 to 97 per cent, FDI inflows to the hotel and tourism sector increased by a very high 328 per cent over the corresponding period in the previous year.

The government has taken many policy initiatives to liberalise the FDI policy for the services sector. These include liberalising the policy on foreign investment for companies operating in the broadcasting sector, like increasing the foreign investment limit from 49 per cent to 74 per cent in teleports (setting up up-linking HUBs/teleports) and direct to home (DTH)

Table 5.2: Largest FDI-attracting Services Sector (2005-2013) (Rs. Crore)

Service Sector	2005-06	2006-07	2007-08	2008-09	2009-10	2010-11	2011-12	2012-13	2013-14	Cumulative Inflows (Apr. 2000 to 2013)
Services Sector (Financial and Non-financial)	2399	21047	26589	28516	199945	15054	24656	26306	1291	173567
Construction Development: Township, Housing, Infrastructure	N.A.	N.A.	N.A.	N.A.	N.A.	7590	15236	7248	173	101222
Telecommunications (Radio Paging Cellular Mobile Basic Telephone Services)	2776	2155	5103	11727	12270	7542	9012	1654	33	22112
Hotel and Tourism	64	401	5729	1931	1297	1405	4754	17777	12623	33439
Construction Activities (Including Roads and Highways)	667	4424	6989	8792	13469	N.A.	N.A.	N.A.	N.A.	N.A.
Housing & Real Estate	171	2121	8749	12621	14027	N.A.	N.A.	N.A.	N.A.	N.A.

Source: DIPP (2012-13), Ministry of Commerce and Industry, Government of India.

and cable networks, and permitting foreign investment (FI) of up to 49 per cent in mobile TV; permitting foreign airlines to include foreign investment of up to 49 per cent in scheduled and non-scheduled air transport services; permitting FDI of up to 51 per cent in multi-brand retail trading, and amendment of the existing policy on FDI in single-brand product retail trading.

Review of Literature

An investigation of the intensity of international technology transfer in selected ASEAN economies, viz. Singapore, Malaysia, Thailand, and Indonesia, through the import of machinery and FDI (Lee Huay Huay and Tan Hui Boon 2006, 394-410) indicated that Malaysia and Singapore were the most successful among the selected ASEAN countries in tapping the benefits of FDI and technological transfers with good strategies and policies after the 1998 crisis. In contrast, Indonesia has faced a continuing outflow of FDI since the crisis, leading to a negative impact on its economy.

The long-held policy assumption that aid and FDI serve as complements in accelerating the development of the world's poorer countries has been challenged by Kosack, Stephen and Jennifer Tobin (2006). They showed both theoretically and empirically that aid and FDI affect development differently. Aid contributes powerfully to both economic growth and human development. By contrast, FDI has at best no effect on economic growth and actually slows the rate of human development in less-developed countries.

Soysa and Neumayer (2005) conducted a study to estimate the effects of dependence on trade, FDI and an index of economic freedom on the World Bank's measure of sustainability (the genuine savings rate), which measures the rate at which investment in the total stock of manufactured, human, and natural capital exceeds its depreciation. Their indicators of economic openness showed positive effects on sustainability. They suggested that if increasing trade, FDI, and economic freedom are hallmarks of globalisation, then worries about its effects on future well-being are misplaced.

Andrés López and Daniel Chudnovsky (2008) concluded that FDI was not a panacea for Argentina's economy in the 1990s, but also has not been the chief cause of social problems such as unemployment, increasing income inequality, or environmental degradation. However, they suggested that from the evidence, it appears that Argentina missed the opportunity to reap significant benefits from the large FDI inflows that the country received in the last decade. According to them, while TNC affiliates showed better microeconomic performance than local firms, the latter reaped almost no spillover benefits from foreign presence.

Need and the objectives of the study

In section one, it has been observed firstly that the largest contribution to the growth of GDP has come from the services sector. Second, FDI inflow was high in the services sector during 2000-2011. Third, the trade balance is also positive in services, which provides a cushion to the negative balance of merchandise trade. Last but the not least, the employment rate has risen significantly in the services sector in urban as well as rural India.

By looking at the above results, it can be inferred that FDI in India has played a catalytic role in promoting the growth rate, export and employment. Hence, a study has been conducted to assess the role of FDI in terms of promoting growth in the long run. There is a certain threat of the crowding-out of domestic investment by FDI in the long run. If the growth in the services sector is not linked with the agriculture and manufacturing sectors, it will adversely affect the sustainable growth of the economy.

An attempt has been made to identify the changes in the pattern of FDI inflows into the services sector, especially after the 2007-08 global financial crisis, and to analyse the consistency in FDI inflows. If there is inconsistency in FDI inflows, then there may be unpredictable threats to the long-run sustainability of the economy.

Methodology and Data

To conduct the study, data on the growth rate of GDP (GGDP), FDI, Gross Capital Formation Rate (GCFR), which is used as proxy for domestic investment, export and employment from 2000-2012 were collected from various reports and publications published by the Reserve Bank of India (RBI), the Central Statistical Organisation (CSO), the Department of Industrial Policy and Promotion (DIPP), various issues of the Economic Survey of India and World Bank data.

The empirical analysis was conducted on the basis of various time-series tests, such as the unit root test, panel regression analysis, the Granger causality test and the co-integration test in E-views. The ratio analysis was conducted on FDI/GDP, GCFR/GDP and GGDP. The ratio of FDI/GDP indicates the proportion or contribution of FDI to GDP. Similarly, the ratio of GCFR/GDP indicates proportion or contribution of GCFR to GDP.

Empirical Analysis

It is imperative to observe the patterns and trends in FDI inflows and its corresponding impact on the growth rate of GDP (GGDP) and GCFR in the services sector during 2000-11. The service sector is classified into 1) finance, insurance, real estate and business services, 2) construction, 3) trade, hotels, transport and communication and 4) community, social and personal services.

Finance, Insurance, Real Estate and Business Services

Financial and non-financial services, namely insurance, real estate and business services, which account for the largest FDI inflows, faced deceleration after 2010. It is evident from Tables 5.1 and 5.2, above, and Table 5.3, below, that the FDI/GDP and GCFR/GDP ratios declined during the post-crisis period (2008-09 onwards). However, while the growth rate of GDP (GGDP) showed signs of recovery during 2009-10, it declined sharply from 2010-11 onwards, which shows that this sector is finding it difficult to maintain its earlier pace of growth. A badly affected manufacturing sector, the recession and an alarmingly high unemployment rate have affected the financial and non-financial services sector.

Table 5.3: Development Ratios of Finance, Insurance, Real Estate & Business Services (Rs. Crore)

Year	GCFR	FDI	GDP	GCFR/GDP	FDI/GDP	GGDP
1999-00	N.A	N.A.	233549	N.A.	N.A.	N.A.
2000-01	79,976	320	243048	0.3291	0.0013	0.0407
2001-02	1,09,135	1063	260737	0.4186	0.0041	0.0728
2002-03	1,03,662	1424	281550	0.3682	0.0051	0.0798
2003-04	1,02,148	1194	297250	0.3436	0.0040	0.0558
2004-05	90,465	2610	323080	0.2800	0.0081	0.0869
2005-06	1,08,041	2340	359888	0.3002	0.0065	0.1139
2006-07	1,09,250	18622	409472	0.2668	0.0455	0.1378
2007-08	1,26,282	28615	457584	0.2760	0.0625	0.1175
2008-09	1,65,649	30423	493356	0.3358	0.0617	0.0782
2009-10	1,60,254	27429	538768	0.2974	0.0509	0.0920
2010-11	166048	13046	592061	0.2805	0.0220	0.0989

Source: GCFR (2012-13) Central Statistical Organisation, Govt. of India
FDI (2012-13) DIPP, Factsheet of FDI, Govt. of India
GDP (2012-13) RBI, Handbook of Statistics on Indian Economy, Govt. of India

Construction

Construction is included as part of the services sector by the RBI as well as by the World Bank. FDI to construction was allowed only after 2004-05. It is evident from Table 5.1 and Table 5.2 that FDI, the growth rate of GDP and GCFR all declined after 2009. This decline could be attributed to the recession, high unemployment, and tough preventative action against the illegal mining of sand.

Table 5.4: Development Ratios of Construction at Factor Cost (in Rs. Crore)

Year	GCFR	FDI	GDP	GCFR/GDP	FDI/GDP	GGDP
1999-00	N.A.	N.A.	102007	N.A.	N.A.	N.A.
2000-01	9,074	0	108362	0.0837	0	0.0623
2001-02	15,846	0	112692	0.1406	0	0.04
2002-03	16,947	0	121650	0.1393	0	0.0795
2003-04	21,324	0	136224	0.1565	0	0.1198
2004-05	25,577	508	158212	0.1617	0.0032	0.1614
2005-06	33,217	464	183868	0.1807	0.0025	0.1622
2006-07	41,667	2873	205543	0.2027	0.014	0.1179
2007-08	48,366	4204	226325	0.2137	0.0186	0.1011
2008-09	40,636	4880	242577	0.1675	0.0201	0.0718
2009-10	47,445	7239	259617	0.1827	0.0279	0.0702
2010-11	56,641	2486	280560	0.2019	0.0089	0.0807

Source: GCFR (2012-13) Central Statistical Organisation, Govt. of India
FDI (2012-13) DIPP, Factsheet of FDI, Govt. of India
GDP (2012-13) RBI, Handbook of Statistics on Indian Economy, Govt of India

Trade, Hotels, Transport and Communication

However, as shown in Table 5.5, the hotel and tourism sector has improved because of improvements in telecom connectivity, social, personal and community services such as medical tourism (ayurvedic treatment, better but less costly allopathic treatment), educational institutions, the film industry, demand for foreign artists, etc.

Table 5.5: Development Ratios of Trade, Hotels, Transport and Communication (Rs. Crore)

Year	GCFR	FDI	GDP	GCFR/GDP	FDI/GDP	GGDP
1999-00	N.A.	N.A.	387515	N.A.	N.A.	N.A.
2000-01	1,37,652	2091	415650	0.331	0.005	0.073
2001-02	1,80,536	5420	453847	0.398	0.012	0.092
2002-03	1,82,308	3525	496691	0.367	0.007	0.094
2003-04	1,82,730	2307	556370	0.328	0.004	0.120
2004-05	1,89,224	1606	615849	0.307	0.003	0.107
2005-06	2,05,947	3869	690399	0.298	0.006	0.121
2006-07	2,20,011	5552	778896	0.282	0.007	0.128
2007-08	2,61,174	15755	875398	0.298	0.018	0.124
2008-09	2,98,248	22967	954589	0.312	0.024	0.090
2009-10	3,09,182	17905	1047370	0.295	0.017	0.097
2010-11	3,33,577	11536	1154780	0.289	0.010	0.103

Source: GCFR (2012-13) Central Statistical Organisation, Govt. of India
FDI (2012-13) DIPP, Factsheet of FDI, Govt. of India
GDP (2012-13) RBI, Handbook of Statistics on Indian Economy, Govt. of India

India's telecommunication network is the second largest in the world, based on the total number of telephone users (both fixed and mobile phones). However, it has been observed that until 2011-12, most mobile phones were foreign made, such as Blackberry (Canada), Lenovo (China), Nokia (Finland), Panasonic (Japan), LG and Samsung (South Korea), Apple and Motorola Mobility (USA), while India's mobile manufacturing companies, such as Beetel, Karbonn and XOLO, were operating at very low levels due to poor quality products and services. However, since 2011-12, this scenario has changed substantially and Indian companies such as Micromax and Karbonn have penetrated the market vigorously and succeeded in replacing foreign competitors.

Community, Social and Personal Services

It is evident from Table 5.6 that the FDI/GDP ratio declined drastically during the post-crisis period in the community, social and personal services sector. The GCFR/GDP ratio and GGDP showed positive change during the same period.

Table 5.6: Development Ratios of Community, Social and Personal Services (Rs. Crore)

Year	GCFR	FDI	GDP	GCFR/GDP	FDI/GDP	GGDP
1999-00	N.A.	N.A.	266707	N.A.	N.A.	N.A.
2000-01	57,676	0	279239	0.207	0.000	0.047
2001-02	71,401	0	290715	0.246	0.000	0.041
2002-03	78,646	0	302153	0.260	0.000	0.039
2003-04	80,582	0	318514	0.253	0.000	0.054
2004-05	98,759	103	340266	0.290	0.000	0.068
2005-06	97,906	133	364313	0.269	0.000	0.071
2006-07	1,10,761	293	385118	0.288	0.001	0.057
2007-08	1,34,892	834	411256	0.328	0.002	0.068
2008-09	1,32,599	1346	464926	0.285	0.003	0.131
2009-10	1,48,928	533	519965	0.286	0.001	0.118
2010-11	167528	716	556385	0.301	0.001	0.070

Source: GCFR (2012-13) Central Statistical Organisation, Govt. of India
FDI (2012-13) DIPP, Factsheet of FDI, Govt. of India
GDP (2012-13) RBI, Handbook of Statistics on Indian Economy, Govt. of India

It is a sign of sustainable economic development that domestic investment in hitherto neglected sectors like education, health and human resource services has remained unaffected, and, in fact, has improved during the post-crisis period.

Testing the crowding in and crowding out impact of FDI on services

With intensifying FDI, there is the possibility of the crowding out or crowding in of domestic investment. Crowding out means that the percentage or proportionate share of domestic industries is reduced in comparison to foreign industries. In this process, foreign industries take maximum advantage of local resources; physical, financial and human. On the contrary, if FDI plays a complementary role to domestic investment, this is called crowding in.

For testing the crowding in and crowding out impacts of FDI on the services sector, the following regression, which was developed by Agosin and Mayor (2002), is used for panel data analysis.

$\frac{GCFR}{GDP_t}\text{Services} = \alpha + \sum_{i=t-i}^{t} \frac{FDI}{GDP} + \sum_{t-j}^{t-1} \frac{GCFR}{GDP} + \sum_{t-k}^{t} GGDP$(i, j and k = 0 to n lags) .... (1.1)

The GCFR/GDP ratio indicates the contribution of gross capital formation (i.e. domestic investment) to GDP growth rate. The FDI/GDP ratio indicates the contribution of FDI to GDP, and GGDP indicates the growth rate of GDP. The lag length of each ratio is tested by carrying out a stationarity test. The results are given in Appendix 5.1.

All sub-sectors of the services sector have been grouped together to check the panel unit root test and panel regression analysis for FDI/GDP, GCFR/GDP and GGDP during the period of 2000-10.

Panel Unit Root Test for the Services sector

To decide the lag length and stationarity of the given variables/ratios, the panel unit root test is done in E-views. The following are the results of the panel unit root test.

- GGDP is stationary at first difference; hence, first lag is considered (Appendix. 5.1. a)
- GCFR:GDP is stationary at first difference; hence lag one is considered (Appendix 5.1.b)
- FDI:GDP is stationary at first difference; hence lag one is considered (Appendix 5.1.c)

Hence, the regression equation based on SIC and the stationarity test is as follows:

$$GCFR/GDP_t = \alpha + \beta_1 GCFR / GDP_{t-1} + \beta_2 FDI / GDP_t + \beta_3 FDI / GDP_{t-1} + \beta_4 GGDP_t + \beta_5 GGDP_{t-1} + \varepsilon \quad \text{.................. (1.2)}$$

The results obtained by processing the data in E-views using multiple regression analysis are presented in Table 5.7.

Table 5.7: Econometric Analysis of Services Sector

Dependent Variable: GCF_GDP				
Method: Panel Least Squares				
Sample (adjusted): 2001 2009				
Cross-sections included: 4				
Total panel (balanced) observations: 36				
Variable	**Coefficient**	**Std. Error**	**t-Statistic**	**Prob.**
FDI_GDP	-0.9250	0.8278	-1.1174	0.2727
FDI_GDPT_1	0.8238	0.8843	0.9316	0.3590
GCF_GDPT_1	0.9555	0.0529	18.0537	0.0000
GGDP	-0.2364	0.2237	-1.0571	0.2989
GGDPT_1	0.0727	0.2252	0.3227	0.7492
C	0.0307	0.0244	1.2559	0.2189

R-squared	0.9262	Mean dependent var.	0.2031
Adjusted R-squared	0.9139	S.D. dependent var.	0.1151
S.E. of regression	0.0338	Akaike info criterion	-3.7868
Sum squared resid.	0.0342	Schwarz criterion	-3.5229
Log likelihood	74.1628	F-statistic	75.2796
Durbin-Watson stat	2.0253	Prob. (F-statistic)	0.0000

From the results of the panel regression analysis in Table 5.7, it is evident that the model attributes 92 per cent (R^2 is 0.92) of variation in the services sector's domestic investment to FDI/GDP and GGDP. The F statistic is 75.27, and the probability of F statistics is 0, which shows that the results are statistically significant. The Durbin-Watson statistic of 2.02 (greater than 2) indicates that there is no serial correlation among variables in the data. Among the independent variables, GCFR/GDP $_{t-1}$ is statistically significant and has a very high coefficient of 0.95.

Testing the Crowding Impact of FDI on the Services Sector

From Table 5.7, we substitute the coefficients in regression equation 1.2 as follows:

$$GCFR/GDP_t = \alpha + \beta_1 FDI / GDP_t + \beta_2 FDI / GDP_{t-1} + \beta_3 GCFR / GDP_t + \beta_4 GGDP_t + \beta_5 GGDP_{t-1} + \varepsilon \quad \text{.................. (1.3)}$$

$$GCFR/GDP_t = 0.03 - 0.92 FDI / GDP_t + 0.82 FDI / GDP_{t-1} + 0.95 GCFR / GDP_{t-1} - 0.23 GGDP_t + 0.07 GGDP_{t-1} + \varepsilon \quad \text{.................. (1.4)}$$

The coefficient of crowding in and crowding out is as follows:

$$\beta = \frac{\sum_i^k \frac{FDI}{GDP}}{1-\sum_i^k \frac{GCFR}{GDP}} \quad \text{.................. (1.5)}$$

$$\beta = \frac{-0.92+0.82}{1-0.95} = -2.27648 \quad \text{.................. (1.6)}$$

$$\beta = -2.27 \quad \text{.................. (1.7)}$$

Inference

β is the coefficient of the long-term impact of FDI on domestic investment. As mentioned above, there are three possible interpretations of β:

- If β =1, then it has no impact.
- If β > 1, then it has a crowding in impact.
- If β < 1, then it implies a crowding out impact.

In this case, the value of β is -2.27, which is less than 1. Hence, the impact of FDI on the services sector is negative. It shows a crowding out impact. In other words, Re.1 of FDI resulted in a reduction in domestic investment of Rs.2.27 in the services sector in India from 2000-2010.

Granger Causality Test between FDI and GCFR

The purpose of performing the Granger causality test is to check the causal relationship between FDI, GCFR and GGDP.

Table 5.8: Pair-wise Granger Causality Test

Sample: 1 44			
Lags: 2			
Null Hypothesis:	**Obs.**	**F-Statistic**	**Probability**
No causal relationship between GCFR and FDI	42	1.81844	0.17648
No causal relationship between FDI and GCFR		5.34406	0.00914
No causal relationship between GDP and FDI	42	2.24323	0.12036
No causal relationship between FDI and GDP		5.37344	0.00894
No causal relationship between GDP and GCFR	42	0.59377	0.55742
No causal relationship between GCFR and GDP		1.06965	0.3535

The results in Table 5.8 show that Hypothesis 2 and Hypothesis 4 can be rejected at the 5 per cent level of significance. This shows that there is a causal relationship between FDI and GCFR, as well as GDP, in the services sector. This shows clear cut dominance of FDI in determining GCFR, i.e. domestic investment, as well as the GDP growth rate.

Co-integration Test

In order to check the co-integration or the long-run association between FDI, GCFR and GGDP, the Johansen co-integration test was run. The result is as follows:

Table 5.9: Co-integration Test Result*

Sample (adjusted): 3 44				
Included observations: 42 after adjustments				
Trend assumption: Linear deterministic trend				
Series: FDI GCFR GDP				
Lags interval (in first differences): 1 to 1				
Unrestricted Co-integration Rank Test (Trace)				
Hypothesised		Trace	0.05	
No. of CE(s)	**Eigen value**	**Statistic**	**Critical Value**	**Prob.****
None *	0.351517	36.44985	29.79707	0.0074
At most 1 *	0.298117	18.25882	15.49471	0.0187
At most 2	0.077571	3.391274	3.841466	0.0655
Trace test indicates 2 co-integrating eqn(s) at the 0.05 level				
* denotes rejection of the hypothesis at the 0.05 level				
**MacKinnon-Haug-Michelis (1999) p-values				

* Full result is in Appendix 5.2

The co-integration result in Table 5.9 shows that there is a long-run relationship between FDI, GCFR and GDP.

Concluding Remarks

It has been observed that FDI in India has no consistent pattern. However, certain sectors are considered to be favoured by MNCs, viz. financial and non-financial services, IT and FMCG. From the above analysis, we can conclude that FDI had a crowding-out effect on the services sector in India during 1999-2011. Similarly, it has been observed that there is a causal relationship between FDI and GCFR and GDP, which shows the clear dominance of FDI in the services sector.

References

Agosin, Manuel and Ricardo Mayer. 2000. "Foreign Investment in Developing Countries, Does it Crowd in Domestic Investment?" UNCTAD/OSG/DP/146 http://unctad.org/en/Docs/dp_146.en.pdf

Agosin, Manuel and Roberto Machado. 2005. "Foreign Investment in Developing Countries: Does it Crowd in Domestic Investment?" *Oxford Development Studies,* Taylor and Francis Journals. Vol. 33(2). Pp. 149-162.

Andrés López and Daniel Chudnovsky. 2008. "Foreign Investment and Sustainable Development in Argentina". Discussion Paper Number 12. Working Group on Development and Environment in the Americas. Pp. 1-24.

Government of India. 2013. *Economic Survey 2012–13*. Chapter 10, Pp: 1, 213, 215. New Delhi: Ministry of Finance.

Homlong Nathalie and Elisabeth Springler. 2010. "Economic Development and Foreign Direct Investment: How to Create Sustainable Development: An Analysis of the Potential for Sustainable Development on the Indian Subcontinent." *Panoeconomicus, Scientific Review*, Vol. 3. Pp. 333-347.

Kosack, Stephen and Jennifer Tobin. 2006. "Funding Self-Sustaining Development: The Role of Aid, FDI and Government in Economic Success." *International Organisation*, Vol. 60, issue 1. Pp 205-243.

Lee Huay Huay and Tan Hui Boon. 2006. "Financial Issues in the Asia-Pacific Region, Technology Transfer, FDI and Economic Growth in the ASEAN Region." *Journal of the Asia Pacific Economy*, Vol. 11, issue 4. Pp. 394-410.

Soysa, Indra D. and Eric Neumayer. 2005. "False Prophet or Genuine Savior? Assessing the Effects of Economic Openness on Sustainable Development, 1980-99." *International Organisation*, Vol. 59, issue 3. Pp. 731-772.

Appendix 5.1

Appendix 5.1 (a) Services Sector – Unit Root Test (lag 1) GGDP				
Panel unit root test: Summary Sample: 2000 2009 Exogenous variables: None User specified lags at: 1 Newey-West bandwidth selection using Bartlett kernel Balanced observations for each test				
Method	**Statistic**	**Prob.****	**Cross-sections**	**Obs**
Null: Unit root (assumes common unit root process)				
Levin, Lin & Chu t*	-5.51979	0	4	28
Breitung t-stat	-1.82858	0.0337	4	24
Null: Unit root (assumes individual unit root process)				
ADF - Fisher Chi-square	34.4736	0	4	28
PP - Fisher Chi-square	36.7749	0	4	32
** Probabilities for Fisher tests are computed using an asymptotic Chi-square distribution. All other tests assume asymptotic normality.				

Appendix 5.1 (b) Services Sector – Unit Root Test (lag 1) GCFR/GDP				
Panel unit root test: Summary Sample: 2000 2009 Exogenous variables: None User specified lags at: 1 Newey-West bandwidth selection using Bartlett kernel Balanced observations for each test				
Method	**Statistic**	**Prob.****	**Cross-sections**	**Obs**
Null: Unit root (assumes common unit root process)				
Levin, Lin & Chu t*	-8.82366	0	4	28
Breitung t-stat	-2.75283	0.003	4	24
Null: Unit root (assumes individual unit root process)				
ADF - Fisher Chi-square	37.6397	0	4	28
PP - Fisher Chi-square	58.3046	0	4	32
** Probabilities for Fisher tests are computed using an asymptotic Chi-square distribution. All other tests assume asymptotic normality.				

Appendix 5.1 (c) Services Sector – Unit Root Test (lag 1) FDI/GDP				
Panel unit root test: Summary Sample: 2000 2009 Exogenous variables: None User specified lags at: 1 Newey-West bandwidth selection using Bartlett kernel Balanced observations for each test				
Method	**Statistic**	**Prob.****	**Cross-sections**	**Obs**
Null: Unit root (assumes common unit root process)				
Levin, Lin & Chu t*	-3.74439	0.0001	4	28
Breitung t-stat	-0.27644	0.3911	4	24
Null: Unit root (assumes individual unit root process)				
ADF - Fisher Chi-square	20.3387	0.0091	4	28
PP - Fisher Chi-square	19.5164	0.0123	4	32
** Probabilities for Fisher tests are computed using an asymptotic Chi-square distribution. All other tests assume asymptotic normality.				

Appendix 5.2

Appendix 5.2: Co-integration Test				
Sample (adjusted): 3 44				
Included observations: 42 after adjustments				
Trend assumption: Linear deterministic trend				
Series: FDI GCFR GDP				
Lags interval (in first differences): 1 to 1				
Unrestricted Co-integration Rank Test (Trace)				
Hypothesized		Trace	0.05	
No. of CE(s)	**Eigen value**	**Statistic**	**Critical Value**	**Prob.****
None *	0.351517	36.44985	29.79707	0.0074
At most 1 *	0.298117	18.25882	15.49471	0.0187
At most 2	0.077571	3.391274	3.841466	0.0655
Trace test indicates 2 co-integrating eqn(s) at the 0.05 level				
* denotes rejection of the hypothesis at the 0.05 level				
**MacKinnon-Haug-Michelis (1999) p-values				
Unrestricted Co-integration Rank Test (Maximum Eigen value)				
Hypothesized		Max-Eigen	0.05	
No. of CE(s)	**Eigen value**	**Statistic**	**Critical Value**	**Prob.****
None	0.351517	18.19104	21.13162	0.1229
At most 1 *	0.298117	14.86754	14.2646	0.0401
At most 2	0.077571	3.391274	3.841466	0.0655
Max-Eigen value test indicates no co-integration at the 0.05 level				
* denotes rejection of the hypothesis at the 0.05 level				
**MacKinnon-Haug-Michelis (1999) p-values				
Unrestricted Co-integrating Coefficients (normalized by b'*S11*b=I):				
FDI	GCFR	GDP		
7.15E-05	6.03E-05	-2.03E-05		
0.00011	-2.70E-05	8.65E-06		
6.77E-05	-8.67E-06	-2.32E-06		

Unrestricted Adjustment Coefficients (alpha):				
D(FDI)	-1266.94	-2110.114	-76.72372	
D(GCFR)	392.4169	-11719.41	11452.11	
D(GDP)	22371.39	-43056.31	31231.23	
1 Co-integrating Equation(s):		Log likelihood	-1415.945	
Normalized co-integrating coefficients (standard error in parentheses)				
FDI	GCFR	GDP		
1	0.844433	-0.284125		
	-0.20773	-0.06794		
Adjustment coefficients (standard error in parentheses)				
D(FDI)	-0.09054			
	-0.04981			
D(GCFR)	0.028043			
	-0.54497			
D(GDP)	1.59873			
	-1.64965			
2 Co-integrating Equation(s):		Log likelihood	-1408.511	

Normalized co-integrating coefficients (standard error in parentheses)				
FDI	GCFR	GDP		
1	0	-0.003069		
		-0.00833		
0	1	-0.332834		
		-0.01552		

Adjustment coefficients (standard error in parentheses)				
D(FDI)	-0.323322	-0.019497		
	-0.07946	-0.03996		
D(GCFR)	-1.264811	0.340018		
	-0.96984	-0.48778		
D(GDP)	-3.15113	2.512222		
	-2.88801	-1.45251		

CHAPTER SIX

FDI IN THE AVIATION SECTOR: CHALLENGES AND THE ROAD AHEAD

RUCHI BHANDARI

The Vision

The vision for the Indian civil aviation industry for the 12th Plan period is:

> "To propel India among the top five civil aviation markets in the world by providing access to safe, secure and affordable air services to everyone through an appropriate regulatory framework and by developing world class infrastructure facilities."[1]

According to the International Air Transport Association's (IATA) Airline Industry Forecast 2012-16, India's domestic air travel market will be among top five globally, experiencing the second highest growth rate, at a compounded annual growth rate (CAGR) of 13.1 per cent. In order to facilitate this significant growth potential and to achieve the vision of the Indian civil aviation industry, India will need more airports, higher capacity, supporting infrastructure, finance and human resources. All this would require a progressive and positive fiscal regime and policies and a collaborative approach between the government and the industry.

Introduction to the Present Regime of Foreign Direct Investment (FDI) Policy in the Indian Airline Industry

Circular 1 of 2012 of the Consolidated FDI Policy, effective from April 10th, 2012, relating to air transport services, stated that no foreign airlines were allowed to participate directly or indirectly in the equity of an

---

[1] Planning Commission of India. 2011.

air transport undertaking engaged in operating scheduled or non-scheduled air transport services except cargo airlines.

In a major move for the aviation sector, in Press Note 6 of the 2012 Series, the government reviewed its FDI policy on aviation and decided to permit foreign airlines to invest in the capital of Indian airline companies operating scheduled and non-scheduled air transport services up to a limit of 49 per cent of their paid-up capital.[2] Press Note 6 laid down the following conditions with respect to FDI in airlines sector:

(a) Air transport services include domestic scheduled passenger airlines,[3] non-scheduled air transport services,[4] helicopter and seaplane services.

(b) Foreign airlines are allowed to participate in the equity of companies operating cargo airlines, helicopter and seaplane services, as per the limits and entry routes mentioned above.

(c) Foreign airlines are also henceforth allowed to invest in the capital of Indian companies operating scheduled and non-scheduled air transport services up to the limit of 49 per cent of their paid-up capital. Such investment is subject to the following conditions:

(i) It must be made through the approved route.

(ii) The 49 per cent limit will subsume FDI and FII (foreign institutional investor) investment.

(iii) Investments made in this way need to comply with the relevant regulations of the Securities and Exchange Board of India (SEBI), such as the Issue of Capital and Disclosure Requirements (ICDR) Regulations/Substantial Acquisition of Shares and Takeovers (SAST) Regulations, as well as other applicable rules and regulations.

(iv) A scheduled operator's permit can only be granted to a company

- that is registered and has its principal place of business within India
- the chairman and at least two-thirds of the directors of which are citizens of India

---

[2] Department of Industrial Policy and Promotion, Ministry of Commerce and Industry, Government of India. 2012. "Press Note No. 6 (2012 Series)".

[3] "Scheduled air transport service" means an air transport service undertaken between the same two or more places and operated according to a published timetable or with flights so regular or frequent that they constitute a recognizably systematic series, all flights being open to use by members of the public.

[4] "Non-scheduled air transport service" means any service which is not a scheduled air transport service, and includes cargo airlines.

- the substantial ownership and effective control of which is vested in Indian nationals.

(v) All foreign nationals likely to be associated with Indian scheduled and non-scheduled air transport services as a result of such investment must be cleared from a security point of view before deployment and

(vi) All technical equipment that might be imported into India as a result of such investment will require clearance from the relevant authority in the Ministry of Civil Aviation.

(d) The policy mentioned in (c), above, is not applicable to M/s Air India Limited.

Although changes have been made in the FDI Policy related to aviation, the country has not been able to harness the potential of liberalization in the aviation sector due to various challenges imposed by regulators, airports, oil marketing companies and policy makers.

The same FDI limit in the civil aviation sector is maintained in the FDI policies of 2013 and 2014.[5] Taking cognizance of the conditions laid down in the FDI Policy 2014 for FDI in the aviation sector, this paper will analyze its impact on the airline industry. The objective of this paper is to analyze the challenges in the path of FDI in the airline industry, suggest measures to overcome these challenges, and identify the gaps between the present state and the desired state of the Indian civil aviation industry.

Challenges

In order to achieve its vision, the Indian civil aviation industry is facing various challenges posed by increasing fuel costs, the tax regime, government policies and airport infrastructure issues and, above all, the financial distress faced by the aviation industry. In addition to this, India's civil aviation industry has recently been facing a number of operational challenges due to economic recession and the cyclical[6] nature of its earnings.

---

[5] There have been no changes made in the FDI cap for civil aviation in the FDI policy for the years 2013 and 2014. The status quo is maintained. For further reference, the author will use FDI Policy 2014.

[6] Pierson, K. and Sterman, J. D. 2013.

Tax Regime on Aviation Turbine Fuel (ATF)

Present Situation: The rising cost of ATF, coupled with the depreciation of the rupee, cuts into the profits of the airline industry. ATF costs contribute 30-45 per cent of overall operating costs for full service carriers (FSCs) and 40-55 per cent for low cost carriers (LCCs).[7] The estimated annual fuel bill for the industry was around USD 1.7 billion in the year 2013. Domestic ATF prices are linked to fluctuations in crude oil prices and the exchange rate of the rupee against the US Dollar. ATF accounts for nearly half of an Indian carrier's operating cost, compared to 20-25 per cent globally. The airlines industry has been adversely affected by the significant increase in ATF prices (up 57 per cent in the last 18 months) as Indian carriers cannot hedge fuel prices.[8] The under-developed commodity hedging market makes it difficult for airline companies to hedge against the fluctuating prices of ATF. With the steadily increasing price of oil, airlines have no option but to pass on the rising cost of inputs to passengers as much as possible. An urgent reassessment of the present oil/petrol product hedging regulations is needed. Domestic airlines should be permitted to hedge their ATF price risks. Many global airlines use fuel hedging for effective risk management.

Computation of ATF price in India: The price of ATF in India is based on international import parity prices, and directly linked to the benchmark of Platt's publication of FOB Arabian Gulf ATF prices; it is not related to the actual cost of producing it in India. The base price in India is calculated on an import parity basis, which adds shipping costs and insurance to the internationally traded price of jet fuel.

Taxes on ATF prices include a 10 per cent ad valorem customs duty (which adds up to an effective rate of approximately 20 per cent inclusive of the countervailing duty (CVD) and cess), excise duty of 8.24 per cent (including cess) and sales tax (levied by the state governments), averaging 25 per cent across the country, as add-ons to the Arabian Gulf prices.[9]

The additional costs added to the cost of ATF include freight charges from the Gulf to India, domestic transportation and other charges, oil companies' marketing margins and throughput charges paid to the Airports Authority of India.

---

[7] ICRA Ltd. 2012.

[8] ICRA Ltd. 2012.

[9] ICRA Ltd. 2012.

In Delhi, taxes and duties make up around 32 per cent of the final price of the fuel. Currently, ATF sold in the country is nearly 50-60 per cent costlier than in overseas markets like Bangkok, Singapore or Dubai.[10]

Table 6.1: Prices of ATF charged by Indian Oil Marketing Companies (OMCs) in metro cities as of August 01, 2013

City	Duty paid prices before sales tax (Rs/kl)	ATF prices for Domestic Airlines per kilolitre (kl)	ATF Prices for International Airlines per kl
Delhi	Rs 58492.45	USD 987.21 or Rs 70203.15	USD 927.37
Kolkata	Rs 64253.62	USD 1084.45 or Rs 80317.03	USD 966.14
Mumbai	Rs 57982.00	USD 978.60 or Rs 72477.50	USD 978.60
Chennai	Rs 59157.28	USD 998.44 or Rs 76312.90	USD 930.59

Source: Indian Oil Corporation Limited. 2013. "ATF/Jet Fuel"

Table 6.2: Prices of ATF charged by Indian OMCs in metro cities as applicable from midnight of May 31, 2014 and June 01, 2014

City	ATF prices for Domestic Airlines per kilolitre (kl)	ATF Prices for International Airlines per kl
Delhi	Rs 69747.98	USD 917.48 or Rs 54319.4034[11]
Kolkata	Rs 79869.08	USD 958.79 or Rs 56765.1619
Mumbai	Rs 71940.36	USD 920.99 or Rs 54527.212
Chennai	Rs 76049.69	USD 923.57 or Rs 54679.96

Source: Indian Oil Corporation Limited. 2014. "ATF/Jet Fuel"

The difference in prices for domestic and international airlines in metros is evident from the comparisons in the tables above. Indian carriers flying abroad are at a disadvantage compared to foreign airlines, which are exempt from all taxes under the Foreign Aircraft (Duties on Fuel and

---

[10] Hoping to bring down jet fuel prices, fares: Singh 2013.

[11] The exchange rate on May 31st, 2014 for one USD was Rs 59.205, which has been used to convert USD into Rupees.

Lubricants) Act of 2002. Besides this, domestic airlines have to pay value added tax (VAT), from which international airlines are exempt.

Therefore, domestic ATF prices are significantly higher than international benchmarks. This has adversely affected the financial health of India's airlines and FDI in the Indian aviation industry.

Cost of Congestion at Airports

Present Situation: "As long as high taxes prevail, high airport costs and congestion, and poorly developed air navigation (services) means more congestion, high cost of operations exist, you are not going to get a lot of people to invest in airlines,"[12] the Director General and CEO of the International Air Transport Association (IATA) said at his operational headquarters in Geneva on the increase of FDI limits to 49 per cent in the Indian aviation sector.

Air carriers are users of the aviation system – a system composed of airport facilities, air traffic control services, and usable air space – and are the second most significantly affected users of the aviation system. Although air carriers have more direct control over congestion levels, the majority of air carriers can do little independently to control congestion levels. Although reduced congestion would benefit all air carriers, there is little incentive for an individual air carrier to act, as the congestion levels can be reduced by the expansion of the airports by the government. The government will then take back its costs from the airline carriers by levying additional taxes. Therefore, the airline industry has little incentive to act, as it would lead to an increase in costs. Congestion causes delays, which negatively affect airline operations in several ways. Delays during "engines on" periods require additional fuel; all delays require additional crew time; delays require airlines to adjust flight plans, possibly affecting the crews and schedules of subsequent flights, and airlines must maintain sufficient logistics and staffing to respond to regular delays. All of these things impose expenses on airlines, which, as much as possible, they pass on to travellers in ticket prices and additional fees. To estimate the incremental cost of congestion delays to airlines, the types of delay must be matched to the types of expense incurred. High congestion at major airports in India, for example hovering for half an hour at a major airport, could increase fuel costs by between Rs 60,000 and Rs 115,000, depending on the aircraft, as well as affecting aircraft utilization.

[12] FDI will not come to Indian aviation until high costs prevail: IATA Chief Tony Tyler 2012.

Therefore, rather than bearing these costs on a regular basis due to congestion at airports, the aviation sector should push for airport expansion.

Five-Year/20 Aircraft Rule

Present Situation: In India, the Ministry of Civil Aviation has imposed the 5/20 rule, which makes it mandatory for any domestic airline to have a fleet of at least 20 aircraft and a record of five years of domestic operations before it can be allowed to fly overseas.[13] The rationale provided at the time of making the rule was that for the protection of passengers, carriers needed to demonstrate their credentials in the domestic market before being considered capable of handling the additional complexity of international operations. But this restriction discriminated against Indian carriers since it did not apply to foreign airlines.

Impact on competition: While Air Arabia, Etihad and Tiger Airways were granted permission to fly to India despite having been in operation for less than five years at the time of entry, Indian airlines such as Kingfisher, IndiGo and SpiceJet could not fly out. The 5/20 aircraft rule imposed an unnecessary restriction, which only benefited Jet Airways. Indirectly, the 5/20 rule may have been one of the contributory causes to Kingfisher's demise. Its decision to acquire Air Deccan was driven in part by the fact that Deccan was approaching five years of operations and would allow Kingfisher to launch international services.

Airport Tariffs

Present Situation: The tariffs airport operators charge can be divided into two broad categories: landing, parking and housing fees, and 'user development' charges. While the former have to be borne by the airlines, the latter can be passed on to passengers in the form of fares.[14] Airport development fees (ADF) fill a part of the viability gap in funding needed to meet construction costs, while user development fees (UDF) are charged to cover operational costs. Operators also earn from the non-aeronautical opportunities airports offer, such as by leasing space to shops. In addition to ADF and UDF, airports charge airline companies a variety

---

[13] Aviation ministry may move cabinet note to scrap '5-year/20 aircraft' rules, 2014.

[14] Kaushik 2012.

of tariffs, ranging from landing, parking and housing charges, aerobridge charges, fuel throughput charges, and CUTE[15] counter charges.

Table 6.3: ADF and UDF Charges levied at various airports in India (in Indian National Rupees)

Cities	Airport Development Fees		User Development Fees	
	Outbound Domestic	Outbound International	Domestic	International
Delhi	200	1300	195.80	1068
Mumbai	100	600	274	548
Chennai	Nil	Nil	166	667
Kolkata	Nil	Nil	400	1000
Trivandrum			Nil	575
Hyderabad			430	1700
Bengaluru			260	1070
Jaipur			150	1000

Source: Airports Authority of India 2013

The airports in various cities in India are charging exorbitant fees from passengers, which increases the cost of air travel and adversely affects demand. This influences the revenues of airline companies adversely. Foreign airline companies are hesitant to make India a connectivity hub, and this adversely affects inbound FDI. These charges will not benefit airports in the long term, as they could diminish their competitiveness in comparison to regional hubs charging lower and more reasonable rates for similar services.

Comparison with International Airports: State-owned Incheon International Airport is the largest in South Korea, handling 44 million passengers a year. For seven successive years (until 2012), it was rated the best airport worldwide by the Airports Council International lobby group. New airlines operating from Incheon airport in South Korea will get a 100 per cent discount on landing fees in their first year of operation at the airport, followed by a 75 per cent concession for the second year and 50 per cent for the third.[16] If an existing airline adds a new destination from the airport, they offer similar discounts. For increasing frequency on existing routes, the airport gives a 50 per cent discount on landing charges. The Dallas/Fort Worth (DFW) International Airport in the US, owned by

[15] CUTE: Common User Terminal Equipment.

[16] Centre for Aviation 2010.

the cities of Dallas and Fort Worth, is the world's fourth busiest airport and handles 58 million passengers a year. Dallas airport has seven runways, the highest number in the world. The airport has a generous incentivization program, with discounts and two-year rebates on landing charges for new airlines. Dallas Airport has a USD 60,000 marketing fund for airlines to promote the airport as a new destination for the first year. And if it is a new airline, the airport provides USD 250,000 for marketing assistance and another USD 150,000 to promote the destination.

Impact: Malaysian low-fare carrier AirAsia X SdnBhd stopped flights to New Delhi and Mumbai from its Kuala Lumpur hub in March, citing the steep increase in costs at the two facilities.[17] Air Asia's proposed Indian joint venture in partnership with the Tata Group also plans to skip high-cost airports such as Delhi and Mumbai, according to airline executives. Air Asia is planning to make Chennai its operational hub. There was a decline of 5.1 per cent in domestic aircraft movement at Delhi International Airport Limited (DIAL) in April 2013 in comparison with April 2012.[18]

Bilateral Air Service Agreements (BASAs)

Concept: Before an airline can operate international services to another country, the government must first negotiate a treaty level agreement with the destination country's government. These treaties are known as bilateral air services agreements. BASA contain provisions on traffic rights, capacity, designation, ownership and control, tariffs and many other clauses addressing competition policy, safety and security.

Present Situation: India has an open skies policy with the United States of America and the United Kingdom, multilateral agreements with Europe and bilateral air services agreements with countries where it wants reciprocal flights to operate. Although India has entered into 101 BASA with various countries all around the world, there are restrictions in these air agreements related to the frequencies of flights, types of aircraft, seat limit, designation and number of operating airlines. The Government of India has also imposed restrictions on flying the A380 aircraft in Indian skies. The 'type of aircraft' clause in BASA specifically excludes the A380 from all such agreements before January 2014. Recently, in January 2014, India lifted its ban on the jumbo jet Airbus A380 in a move that will allow international airlines to start flying the world's largest passenger

[17] Sanjai 2013.

[18] Airports Authority of India April 2013.

plane to India, but only to four of its airports, namely Delhi, Mumbai, Hyderabad and Bangalore; even this is only after airlines fulfil several conditions.[19]

Highly Leveraged Companies

At present, existing Indian airlines have high debt burdens. Financial expenses constitute a large share of their total expenses, resulting in huge losses. All three companies listed on the stock exchange have incurred heavy losses.

Table 6.4: Financial Results of Listed Airline Companies

All figures are in Rs. crore.
Figures in brackets denote losses.

	March 2013	March 2012	March 2011
	Jet Airways		
Operating Profits	902.93	1851.85	2502.91
Financial Expenses	1118.98	2011.24	1872.72
Reported Net Profit	(485.50)	(1236.10)	9.69
	Kingfisher Airlines		
Operating Profits	N/A	(2158.39)	944.04
Financial Expenses	N/A	1276.34	2340.32
Reported Net Profit	N/A	(2011.24)	(1027.40)
	Spice Jet		
Operating Profits	N/A	(598.37)	505.44
Financial Expenses	N/A	52.26	101.66
Reported Net Profit	N/A	(605.77)	439.68

Source: www.kotaksecurities.com

[19] Ministry of Civil Aviation Press Release 2014.

It is obvious from the financial expenses figures from the financial statements of airline companies that they are highly leveraged and running into heavy losses. Kingfisher Airlines has already been declared bankrupt and its efforts to attract FDI generated no positive results.

Recommendations

Changes in the taxation regime of ATF

According to Chanakya,

> "Taxation should not be a painful process for the people. There should be leniency and caution while deciding the tax structure. Ideally, governments should collect taxes like a honeybee, which sucks just the right amount of honey from the flower so that both can survive. Taxes should be collected in small and not in large proportions."

The government should consider including ATF in the "declared goods"[20] category under the Central Sales Tax (CST) Act. This would imply a uniform sales tax of 5 per cent. It should also consider rationalizing the tax regime, particularly the value added tax (VAT) on ATF, as VAT rates on ATF differ from state to state, ranging from 20 per cent to 30 per cent. ATF for turbo-prop aircraft is categorized as declared goods under the Central Sales Tax Act. The Union Budget 2007-08 also accorded the same benefit to regional jets with a take-off mass of less than 40,000 kg. It may also be mentioned that the revenue from sales tax on ATF contributes only 0.5 per cent to 2 per cent of the total sales tax collection of states, while in terms of the operational costs of the airlines, it accounts for 40 per cent. States such as West Bengal, Jharkhand, Chhattisgarh and Madhya Pradesh have slashed the value added tax on aviation turbine fuel (ATF), the consequence of which has been a big jump in flights, leading to a sharp increase in passenger traffic.[21]

Currently, fuel hedging is allowed only for international fuel uplifts. Domestic airlines which procure ATF through domestic refineries at international prices are not permitted to hedge the commodity risk, since they are not physically importing the commodity.

---

[20] Section 2(c) of Central Sales Tax Act, 1956 defines declared goods as those declared u/s 14 of the CST Act as goods of special importance in inter-state trade or commerce.

[21] Bhattacharya 2014.

In February 2012, the government permitted the direct import of ATF by or on behalf of Indian carriers as the actual users and on an actual use basis, but it has remained a non-starter due to lack of appropriate infrastructure. With the option to import directly, the effective taxes on ATF will decrease as airlines will pay import duties but be exempt from paying sales tax, resulting in large savings for airlines. However, the challenges in importing, storing and transporting jet fuel will be a major roadblock for airlines because of the monopoly of oil marketing companies on infrastructure at most Indian airports. For sourcing fuel directly, airlines will have no other option but to share existing infrastructure, possibly under a fee-based scheme, with OMCs. The positive news is that LCC IndiGo has started directly importing ATF into southern ports for some of its flights to reduce costs in order to become increasingly competitive against new players, like Tata-Air Asia and Tata-Singapore Airlines (SIA), set to take off soon.[22]

Another factor that could inhibit direct imports of ATF is the fact that airlines will lose out on volume discounts (ranging between 4 and 5 per cent) and the credit period offered by OMCs and will need to pay in cash for direct imports, implying that incremental funding will be required. As a measure of relief, the Reserve Bank of India (RBI) has allowed entities in the aviation sector to raise external commercial borrowings (ECB) for working capital and the refinancing of outstanding working capital rupee loans availed from domestic banks under the approved route.

The Ministry of Civil Aviation should direct OMCs to bring parity to the prices of ATF charged to international airlines and domestic airlines with overseas flights.

Rationalization of the tax regime on ATF will lead to a reduction in operating costs and make the airline industry attractive for equity and debt financing. It may also help existing airline companies wipe out their losses and become profit making companies, and hence help attract FDI.

[22] Sinha 2014.

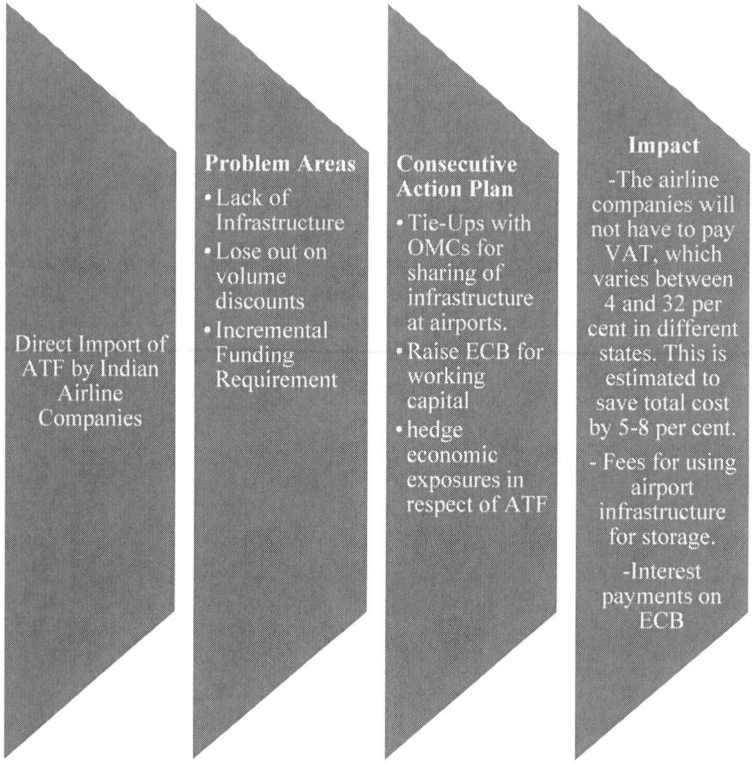

Figure 6.1: Consecutive Action Plan for the direct import of ATF by Indian Airline Companies

Bringing efficiency to air traffic controlling systems at airports

Enhancing and improving communication systems will improve operational decision making and reduce delays. It has been proposed to install a non-voice communications system linking controllers and flight crew (Data Link) and a network-wide communications system linking controllers, pilots and airlines (Net-Centric) to achieve this vision. Airport traffic can be decreased by improved ground movement of airplanes, better techniques for navigation, flight routes that respond to current air traffic demands, clearer communication between pilots and controllers, and improved departure and arrival capacity.

This system has already been adopted at Mumbai International Airport Ltd (MIAL). Delays owing to air traffic have been reduced to about 3-4 per cent of overall departure delays, from 10-12 per cent during 2012, according to the performance reports of the company. The Air Traffic Control department of MIAL has taken various measures, which include strict time allocation for flights, the requirement to request clearance 20 minutes ahead of departure, the introduction of rapid exit taxiways to enable aircraft to clear runways faster and regular on-time performance.[23]

Abolishing the 5 year/20 aircraft Rule

The Civil Aviation Ministry has proposed that this norm be abolished. This is a step in the right direction. This abolition is likely to benefit two new airlines – Air Asia India and Tata-SIA – that would be able to fly internationally from the first day of launch.[24] The government needs to allow new start-up carriers to fly overseas, subject to the availability of bilateral air service agreements and slots, by completely abolishing this rule rather than modifying it.

Changes in ADF and UDF structure

The civil aviation ministry should consider amending aircraft rules to remove UDF from revenue share. This amendment would essentially remove UDF, which is part of the revenue that has to be shared with the Airport Authority of India (AAI) by the airport operator.

New airports have been allotted large acres of land for developing special economic zones for hotels, maintenance, repairs and overhaul (MRO), industry, etc. These airports can raise revenues by charging these industries rent. The airports should look towards raising revenues from non-aeronautical sources to reduce the burden on the airline companies.

Signing Open Skies Agreements

The Government of India should enter into open skies agreements with the governments of other countries. The open skies policy leads to an increase in the output of air transportation services (available seats), a decrease in airline operating expenses, air fare price reductions, and an increase in the demand for air travel (passengers). The Government of

[23] Phadke 2012.

[24] Mishra 2014.

India should modify its BASA with other countries relating to types of aircraft, frequencies and seat limits. The government has permitted airline companies to land their Airbus A380s at Delhi, Mumbai, Bangalore and Hyderabad International Airports from May 30th 2014 onwards, subject to their meeting the bilateral agreements India has with their parent countries.[25] The Government of India should allow more Indian carriers to fly overseas by utilizing the full quota of BASAs. The problems in implementing the open skies policy are related to concerns regarding national security, immigration and ground handling. Open skies agreements may lead to the entry of foreign airline companies by allying with Indian companies.

Conclusion

> "There is nothing wrong with change, if it is in the right direction."
> –Winston Churchill

The Indian Aviation Industry needs leadership, which can be provided by way of the entry of foreign airlines into the Indian market. There is urgent need for more reforms in the Indian aviation sector to maximize FDI inflows and the benefits to passengers, the ailing airline industry, and the economy at large. The challenges detailed in this paper need to be addressed as quickly as possible. Due to the challenges faced by the airline industry, there are not many parties interested in investing in the sector. Many foreign carriers, such as British Airways and Lufthansa, have publicly proclaimed their lack of interest in entering into joint ventures with Indian airline companies because of their lack of profitability and weak fundamentals. Therefore, it is necessary to liberalize the FDI policy and to reform government policies and taxation structures regarding the civil aviation industry further to accommodate foreign airlines as owners and controllers of existing and new airlines in order to achieve the vision for the Indian civil aviation industry for the 12th Plan period.

References

"Airbus A-380s to start flying in and out of India from May 30". 2014. *The Economic Times*. May 7. Accessed June 15, 2014. http://articles.economictimes.indiatimes.com/2014-05-07/news/49689436_1_singapore-airlines-air-services-agreement-sia.

---

[25] Airbus A380s to start flying in and out of India from May 30, 2014.

"Airline Liberalisation". *IATA Economics Briefing No.07*. Accessed August 2013. http://www.iata.org/SiteCollectionDocuments/890000_Airline_Liberalisation_Summary_Report.pdf.

"Aviation ministry may move cabinet note to scrap '5-year/20 aircraft' rules". *The Economic Times*. March 4, 2014. Accessed June 2014. http://articles.economictimes.indiatimes.com/2014-03-04/news/47894734_1_cabinet-note-two-new-airlines-aircraft.

"Economic Survey: Rationalize taxes, introduce fair pricing regime on ATF". 2013. *The Economic Times*. February 27. Accessed July 28, 2013. http://articles.economictimes.indiatimes.com/2013-02-27/news/37330739_1_costs-of-airline-companies-atf-tax-regime.

"FDI won't come to Indian aviation till high costs prevail: IATA chief Tony Tyler". 2012. *The Economic Times*, December 25. Accessed August 16, 2013. http://articles.economictimes.indiatimes.com/2012-12-25/news/35999353_1_tony-tyler-foreign-airlines-indian-carriers.

"Government notifies rules for FDI in aviation, excludes Air India", 2012. *Business Standard*. September 20. Accessed May 24, 2013. http://www.business-standard.com/article/companies/govt-notifies-rules-for-fdi-in-aviation-excludes-air-india-112092000235_1.html.

"Hoping to bring down jet fuel prices, fares: Singh". *The Hindu.* June 30, 2013. Accessed August 14, 2013. http://www.thehindu.com/business/hoping-to-bring-down-jet-fuel-prices-fares-singh/article4866117.ece.

Airports Authority of India. 2013. "Charges for Airports & Air Navigation Services". http://www.aai.aero/misc/AAI-Airport-Charges-updated01072013.pdf.

Airports Authority of India. April 2013. "Traffic Statistics-Domestic Aircraft Movements Annexure-IIB". Accessed December 22. http://www.aai.aero/traffic_news/apr2k13annex2.pdf.

Arushi and Drews, Stefan. 2011. "Aviation and Environment". *Centre for Science and Environment*. 2011. Accessed August 8. http://www.cseindia.org/userfiles/aviation_paper.pdf.

Bhattacharji, Shantanu. 2013. "All you need to know about Jet-Etihad deal". *Business Standard*. April 25. Accessed June 23, 2013. http://www.business-standard.com/article/companies/all-you-need-to-know-about-jet-etihad-deal-113042500357_1.html.

Bhattacharya, Roudra. 2014. "Small-town India takes off with sharp ATF cuts". *The Indian Express*. August 21. Accessed December 10,

2014. http://indianexpress.com/article/business/economy/small-town-india-takes-off-with-sharp-atf-cuts/.

Bhattacharya, Sindhu. 2013. "FDI in aviation: Why not allow foreign airlines to fully own Indian Carriers?" *Firstpost.* June 24. Accessed July 1. http://articles.economictimes.indiatimes.com/2013-02-27/news/37330739_1_costs-of-airline-companies-atf-tax-regime.

CAPA. 2013. "India's airlines lost USD1.65 billion in FY 2013. CAPA India Aviation Outlook 2013/14: Part 4". May 29. Accessed July 26. http://centreforaviation.com/analysis/indias-airlines-lost-usd165-billion-in-fy2013-capa-india-aviation-outlook-201314-part-4-111778.

Centre for Aviation. 2010. "ICN enriches incentive programs for airlines". April 12. Accessed December 9. http://centreforaviation.com/members/direct-news/icn-enriches-incentive-programs-for-airlines-24637.

Chhatrapati Shivaji International Airport. 2013. "Airport Charges-effective FY 2012-13 from 1st April 2013". http://dgca.nic.in/aic/aic2_2013.pdf.

Competition Commission of India. 2013. "Competitive Assessment of Co-operation in the Civil Aviation Industry". Accessed June 2014. http://cci.gov.in/images/media/ResearchReports/Competitive%20Assessment%20of%20Cooperation%20in%20the%20Civil%20Aviation%20Industry.pdf.

Department of Industrial Policy and Promotion, Ministry of Commerce and Industry, Government of India. 2013. "Consolidated FDI Policy: Effective from April 5, 2013". Accessed May 31. http://dipp.nic.in/English/Policies/FDI_Circular_01_2013.pdf.

Department of Industrial Policy and Promotion, Ministry of Commerce and Industry, Government of India. "Press Note No. 6 (2012 Series)". Accessed August 16. http://dipp.nic.in/english/acts_rules/Press_Notes/pn6_2012.pdf

Directorate General of Civil Aviation, Government of India. "Bilateral Air Services Agreements". Accessed July 19. http://dgca.nic.in/bilateral/Bilateral%20-download.pdf.

Downs, Alex, et al. 2012. "The Current State of Indian Aviation: What Indian Airlines need to do to get back in the black". *Air Finance Journal.* September 10. Accessed July 25. http://network.airfinancejournal.com/Post/The-Current-State-of-Indian-Aviation-What-Indian-airlines-need-to-do-to-get-back/6669/True.

FICCI and PwC. 2009. "Indian Aviation: Spreading its wings". February. Accessed July 20.

http://www.ficci.com/spdocument/20216/Changing-Dynamics-Final.pdf.

Ganguly, Nivedita. 2012. "Foreign investment in aviation unlikely to soar for now". *The Hindu Business Line.* September 16. Accessed August 12. http://www.thehindubusinessline.com/industry-and-economy/logistics/foreign-investment-in-aviation-unlikely-to-soar-ornow/article3904450.ece.

IATA. 2012. "Restoring Indian Aviation Competitiveness". Press Release No.:9. March 15. http://www.iata.org/pressroom/pr/pages/2012-03-15-01.aspx.

ICRA Ltd. 2012. "Indian Aviation Industry: Through Turbulent Times, FDI Relaxation not a single game changer". March. Accessed August 20. http://www.icra.in/Files/ticker/Indian%20Aviation%20Industry%20(NEW).pdf.

Indian Oil Corporation Limited. 2014. "ATF/Jet Fuel". Accessed June 24. http://www.iocl.com/Products/AviationTurbineFuel.aspx.

Joshi, Rohit and Vaishnav, Ajay. 2012. "FDI in aviation must be backed with reforms in the sector". *DNA.* September 21. Accessed July 26. http://www.dnaindia.com/money/1743657/report-fdi-in-aviation-must-be-backed-with-reforms-in-the-sector.

Kaushik, Manu. 2012. "Sparks Fly". *Business Today*. September 2. Accessed June 24, 2014. http://businesstoday.intoday.in/story/delhi-airport-charges-dispute-over-steep-hike-grows/1/187212.html.

KPMG. 2013. "Indian Aviation-New Civil Aviation Policy Initiatives", January. Accessed May 31. http://civilaviation.gov.in/cs/groups/public/documents/newsandupdates/moca_001399.pdf.

Ministry of Civil Aviation Press Release. 2014. "Civil Aviation Ministry Approves Operations of Airbus A-380 in India". January 27. Accessed June 18, 2014. http://pib.nic.in/newsite/PrintRelease.aspx?relid=102763.

Ministry of Civil Aviation. "CAPA Comments on Proposed new Civil Aviation Policy". Accessed July 2013. http://civilaviation.gov.in/cs/groups/public/documents/newsandupdates/moca_001398.pdf.

Mishra, Mihir. 2014. "Civil Aviation Ministry to propose abolition of 5/20 rule for domestic airlines to PM". *The Indian Express,* June 2. Accessed June 17, 2014.

http://indianexpress.com/article/business/business-others/civil-aviation-ministry-to-propose-abolition-of-520-rule-for-domestic-airlines-to-pm/.

Mukherjee, Sharmistha. 2013. "AAI to create common infra for direct aviation fuel imports". *Business Standard.* June 7. Accessed August 20. http://www.business-standard.com/article/companies/aai-to-create-common-infra-for-direct-aviation-fuel-imports-113060600692_1.html.

Nathan Economic Consulting India Pvt. Ltd. 2012. "Research Study of the Civil Aviation Sector in India". January. Accessed July 26. http://www.circ.in/pdf/Civil_Aviation_Sector.pdf.

National Council of Applied Economic Research. 2012. "Economic Impact Study of Delhi International Airport". Accessed August 8. http://www.ncaer.org/downloads/Reports/NCAER_Airport%20Report_April_2012.pdf.

Partnership for New York City. 2009. "Grounded: The High Cost of Air Traffic Congestion". February. Accessed August 8. http://www.pfnyc.org/reports/2009_0225_airport_congestion.pdf.

Phadke, Manasi. 2012. "Matter of time: Mumbai airport cuts delays due to traffic congestion by more than half". *The Indian Express.* October 25. Accessed June 16, 2014. http://archive.indianexpress.com/news/matter-of-time-mumbai-airport-cuts-delays-due-to-traffic-congestion-by-more-than-half/1021737/.

Pierson, K. and Sterman, J. D. 2013. "Cyclical dynamics of airline industry earnings". *System Dynamics Review.* 29: 129–156. doi: 10.1002/sdr.1501.

Planning Commission of India. 2011. "Report of Working Group on Civil Aviation for formulation of Twelfth Five Year Plan (2012-17)". Accessed July 25. http://planningcommission.gov.in/aboutus/committee/wrkgrp12/transport/report/wg_civil.pdf.

Reserve Bank of India. 2011. "Comprehensive Guidelines on Foreign Exchange Derivatives and Hedging Commodity Price Risk and Freight Risk Overseas". Accessed August 8. www.rbi.org.in.

Sanjai, P.R. 2013. "Delhi airport may slash user charges next year". *Live Mint.* April 01. Accessed June 17, 2014. http://www.livemint.com/Companies/rYuiPskIgAenQQ2bs5AtzH/Delhi-airport-may-slash-user-charges-next-year.html.

Sinha Saurabh. 2014. "IndiGo starts direct import of jet fuel". *The Times of India.* May 10. Accessed June 16, 2014. http://timesofindia.indiatimes.com/business/india-business/IndiGo-starts-direct-import-of-jet-fuel/articleshow/34902718.cms.

Upadhyay, Anindya and Sikarwar, Deepshikha. 2013. "Comma rescues Air Asia-Tata JV: Strategic position in Press Note 6 ensures clearance". *The Economic Times.* March 7. Accessed July 21. http://articles.economictimes.indiatimes.com/2013-03-07/news/37531757_1_fipb-air-asia-aviation-ministry-officials.

Working Group on Civil Aviation, Planning Commission. 2011. "12th Five-Year Plan for Civil Aviation Sector". Accessed August 20. http://civilaviation.gov.in/cs/groups/public/documents/miscellanous/moca_001320.pdf.

CHAPTER SEVEN

FDI IN RETAIL – THE BANE OF THE INDIAN ECONOMY: A REFERENCE TO GLOBAL IMPACT

SAZZAD PARWEZ AND NEHA SHIVANI

Introduction

Retailing is a global phenomenon today, although it is far more important for a developing economy like India, as it creates employment and boosts the economy. Different people have different definitions of retailing. Retailing is the process of developing, pricing, promoting, and distributing goods and services, which satisfies consumer demand and achieves organizational objectives. The term "retailing", which was previously used as an umbrella term to refer to all commercial transactions, acquired a separate meaning of great significance in the 1990s.

Organized retailing, in India, refers to trading activities undertaken by licensed retailers, that is, those who are registered for sales tax, income tax, etc. These include the publicly traded supermarkets, corporate-backed hypermarkets and retail chains, and also privately owned large retail businesses. Unorganized retailing, on the other hand, refers to the traditional formats of low-cost retailing, for example, local corner shops, owner-manned general stores, *paan/beedi* shops, convenience stores, hand cart and pavement vendors, etc. Organized retailing was absent in most rural and small towns in India in 2010. Supermarkets and similar organized retail accounted for just 4 per cent of the market. The high amount of unorganized retail has been an attractive incentive for Multi-National Companies (MNCs) and corporate houses.

India's retail and logistics industry, organized and unorganized in combination, employs about 40 million Indians (3.3 per cent of the Indian population). Typical Indian retail shops are very small. Over 14 million outlets operate in the country and only 4 per cent of them are larger than

500 square foot (46 m^2) in size. India has about 11 shop outlets for every 1,000 people. Most of the unorganized retail shops in India employ family members, do not have the scale to procure or transport products at a high-volume wholesale level, have limited to no quality control or fake-versus-authentic product screening technology and have staff with no training on safe and hygienic storage, packaging or logistics. Unorganized retail shops source their products from a chain of middlemen, who mark up the product as it moves from the farmer or producer to the consumer. These shops typically offer no after-sales support or service. Finally, most transactions at unorganized retail shops are carried out with cash, with all sales being final.

After the 1980s, India's industrial sector gained in strength and maturity. Its contribution to gross national product (GNP) increased substantially. A new service sector had emerged, signifying the metamorphosis of an agricultural society into an industrial society. Due to the development programs of the central and state governments, service organizations and socially responsible business groups like Mafatlal, Tatas, Birlas, Goenkas and others had taken initiatives to become economically viable and socially relevant and contribute to economic growth. The economic reforms of 1991-92 further accelerated the process of globalization by introducing competition into the markets. There has also been a steady expansion of the rural market for household consumables and durables (Economic Survey 2014).

Retailing is the interface between the producer and the individual consumer buying for personal consumption. This excludes the direct interface between the manufacturer and institutional buyers such as the government and other bulk customers. A retailer is one who stocks the producer's goods and is involved in the act of selling them to the individual consumer at a margin of profit. As such, retailing is the last link that connects the individual consumer with the manufacturing and distribution chain.

Retailing in India is one of the pillars of the economy and accounts for 14 to 15 per cent of the country's gross domestic product (GDP). The Indian retail market is estimated to be worth USD 450 billion and is one of the top five retail markets in the world in terms of economic value. It is also one of the fastest growing retail markets in the world, with 1.2 billion people (Asian Development Bank 2004). India's retailing industry is characterized primarily by small, owner-manned shops. In 2010, larger format convenience stores and supermarkets accounted for about 4 per cent of the industry, and these were present only in large urban centres. India's retail and logistics industry employs about 40 million people (3.3

per cent of the Indian population). Until 2012 the Indian central government prohibited foreign direct investment (FDI) in multi-brand retail, forbidding foreign groups from any ownership in supermarkets, convenience stores or retail outlets. Even single-brand retail was limited to 51 per cent ownership, and bureaucratic delaying activities may not be encouraging enough.

In January 2012, India approved reforms for single-brand stores, welcoming anyone in the world to innovate in the Indian retail market with 100 per cent ownership, but imposed the requirement that single-brand retailers source 30 per cent of their goods from India. In June 2012, IKEA announced that it had applied for permission to invest USD 1.9 billion in India and set up 25 retail stores. According to Fitch (2013), a global rating agency, the 30 per cent requirement is likely to significantly delay if not prevent most single-brand majors from Europe, the USA and Japan from opening stores and creating jobs in India. On December 7th, 2012, the Government of India allowed 51 per cent FDI in multi-brand retail in India. The government managed to get approval for multi-brand retail in parliament, despite strong opposition to the move from opposition parties. Some states allow foreign supermarkets like Walmart, Tesco and many more to open, while other states will not (Arabi 2005).

Objectives of the Study

- To study and understand the concept of foreign direct investment (FDI) in the context of other countries
- To analyze the current status of foreign direct investment (FDI) in retail in India
- To study and understand how foreign direct investment (FDI) in retail can affect the Indian economy

Scope of the Study

The scope of the study is limited to studying the concept of foreign direct investment in the country, how it has affected developing economies and what the road ahead might be in the Indian context. It also focuses on foreign direct investment and its impact on Indian economic development.

Limitations of the Study

The major limitations of the study are the following:

- The paper has been prepared based on data collected from published and unpublished secondary sources.
- The study's findings are based on the limited coverage of selected developing countries.

Retail and Multi Brand Retail in India

Sometime in 1999, the Government of India started mulling over the proposal to permit foreign direct investment in retail trade, which may lead to more organized forms of retailing, employment and productivity, although there had been an earlier decision (1997) not to permit FDI in retail. To an extent, international pressure to open up the retail sector to foreign players played a part in forcing the volte-face. The reasons for foreign investors' interest in the Indian retail sector were obvious. India's retail market is large, with an estimated size of about USD 200-220 billion (approximately Rs.1,000,000 crore). India also has the largest retail density in the world, with about 14 million retail outlets.

The move to allow foreign direct investment in retail met with stiff resistance from several political parties, as well as the trading community. The main rationale offered for the opposition was that allowing FDI in the retail sector would wipe out small retail outlets and contribute significantly to unemployment. In 2007, therefore, the government set up a Parliamentary Standing Committee to look into the issue. In 2009, the committee's report was presented to the Lok Sabha and the Rajya Sabha. It unanimously recommended that FDI in retail should not be permitted. The committee felt that "in a country with huge numbers of people and high level of poverty, the existing model of retailing is most appropriate in terms of economic viability" (PRS Legislative Research Report 2009).

Subsequently, the government published a discussion paper inviting all those interested in the issue to send their views to the Department of Industrial Policy and Promotion (DIPP). This discussion paper listed several advantages of permitting FDI in multi-brand retail – this was in sharp contrast to the unequivocal opposition of the Parliamentary Standing Committee on FDI in retail. The advantages listed included the benefit to consumers by way of lower prices resulting from supply chain efficiency and the better technology of large retailers. CRISIL, in a study conducted in 2012, dismissed many of the advantages attributed to FDI in retailing as "myths created by a few multi-national retail companies" like Walmart, Tesco, Metro GMBH, Carrefour, etc., that were keen to set up shop in India.

International experience appears to counter the claim made by multi-national retail companies that their entry would not adversely affect small retailers. According to McKinsey and Company (2008), and KPMG (2010), the number of small retailers in the UK fell from 56,862 to 25,800. In Europe, four lakh retailers had to close down their establishments during the period 1970-80. The numbers of Indian corner shop retailers in the UK have fallen substantially in the last 10 years. In Thailand, since their entry in 1997, TESCO, Carrefour and Makro have successfully captured more than 10 per cent of the entire retail market. Due to the predatory pricing strategies of corporates, the profit margins for foreign retailers range from –1 per cent to –3 per cent. The pricing war has already started affecting the smaller traditional retailers, who have begun to close their shops. While the introduction of FDI in retail has catalyzed the sector and organized retailing has jumped to more than 40 per cent, many traditional retailers have been rendered unemployed. 60 thousand small retailers have been adversely impacted due to 'predatory pricing' in Thailand. Other Asian countries have had similar experiences. Most countries are now wary of allowing FDI in retail. Indonesia and Malaysia have specified zones within which foreign retailers may operate. In Japan, such retailers need to seek the views of small local stores regarding their proposed location. Additionally, zoning laws have been imposed, compelling foreign retailers to set up shop beyond city limits. Even in the USA, corporate-led investment in organized retail has come up against opposition. City councils in California and Chicago have vetoed the opening of new Walmart stores. There are major reservations even in developed markets (e.g. the USA, France, and Germany) about allowing the unrestrained growth of large format big box discounters. Most of them are not allowed to operate in city centres and have to gain permission from local county and district authorities before they can open new stores (Technopak Projections 1999).

Retail as a 'Forced Employment' Sector

It is important to understand how retailing works in our economy, and what role it plays in the lives of its citizens from a social as well as an economic perspective. India still predominantly houses traditional formats of retailing, that is, local *kirana* shops, paan/beedi shops, hardware stores, weekly *haats*, convenience stores, and bazaars, which together form the bulk of the retail sector. Most importantly, Indian retail is highly fragmented, with about 14 million outlets operating in the country, of which only 4 per cent are larger than 500 square foot in size. Compare this with the figure of just 0.9 million in the USA, catering to more than 13 times the Indian retail market size. According to the global consultancy firms AC Neilsen and KSA Technopak, India has the highest shop density in the world. In 2011, they estimated there were 14 outlets for every 1,000 people.

One of the principal reasons behind the explosion of retail and its fragmented nature in the country is the fact that retailing is probably the primary form of disguised unemployment/underemployment in the country. Given the already overcrowded agriculture sector, a stagnating manufacturing sector, and the hard nature and relatively low wages of jobs in both, many millions of Indians are virtually forced into the services sector. Given the lack of opportunities, it is almost a natural decision for an individual to set up a small shop or store, depending on his or her means and capital. And thus, a retailer is born, seemingly out of circumstance rather than choice. This phenomenon quite aptly explains the millions of kirana shops and small stores. The explosion of retail outlets in the busiest streets of Indian villages and towns is a visible testimony to this. The presence of more than one retailer for every 100 people is indicative of the lack of economic opportunities that is forcing people into this form of self-employment, even though much of it is marginal. Because of this fragmentation, the Indian retail sector typically suffers from limited access to capital, labor and real estate options. The typical traditional retailer follows the low-cost-and-size format, functioning at a small-scale level, rarely liable for tax and following a cheap model of operations.

Retailing is by far the easiest business to enter, with low capital and infrastructure needs, and performs a vital function in the economy as a social security net for the unemployed. India, being a free and democratic country, provides its people with this cushion so they are able to make a living for themselves through self-employment, as opposed to an economy like China, where employment is regulated. Most of these so-called "self-employed" retailers are simply trying to scrape together a living in the face of limited opportunities for employment. In this light, one could brand this sector as one of "forced employment", where the retailer is pushed into it, purely because of the paucity of opportunities in other sectors. Experiences in the US and the EU show that retail giants have destroyed the livelihood of small shopkeepers, who have become employees of such giants.

Trouble for the Farmers

India has experienced remarkable growth in the production of various agricultural commodities over the last four decades. Technological intervention in the late 1960s helped the country, which was wracked by chronic food shortage in the first two decades after independence, become a food grain surplus country. However, more recently, the changing cropping pattern has raised doubts about the sustainability of agricultural production. Another worrisome development has been the emergence of contract farming, which demands strict adherence to quality and volume conditions that food retailers impose on farmers, who earn a reasonable price for the produce as per contract, independent of market fluctuations. It does not allow farmers to realize rising market prices. How will our small tomato or onion farmers cope with the vagaries of the weather and the infrastructural constraints to fulfill their legal contracts? A Food and Agriculture Organization (FAO) paper based on the proceedings[1] of a workshop states: "Farmers experience many problems in supplying supermarkets in Asia and in some cases, this has already been reflected in fairly rapid declines in the numbers involved, as companies tend to delist suppliers who do not come up to expectations in terms of volume, depressed prices due to cut throat competition among the food retailers, delayed payments and lack of credit and insurance." The emergence of such problems in India, especially in the context of the deep crisis that has engulfed the agrarian economy, is entirely avoidable. The MNCs will deal with only the large growers, fix prices in advance and the system of transparent auctions in *Mandis* will be bypassed. Since contract marketing talks about the pre-agreed prices of produce in advance, farmers may find themselves bound to accept these prices even if market prices are higher than the pre-agreed prices.

Global Experience and Perspective

In February 2008, a large number of members of the European Union (EU) Parliament adopted a declaration stating that "throughout the EU, retailing is increasingly dominated by a small number of supermarket chains. Evidence from across the EU suggests large supermarkets are

[1] Shepherd, A.W. (2004), "The implications of supermarket development for horticultural farmers and traditional marketing systems in Asia", paper presented at FAO/AFMA/FAMA Regional Workshop on The Growth of Supermarkets as Retailers of Fresh Produce, Kuala Lumpur, October 4-7, 2004.

abusing their buying power to force down prices paid to suppliers to unsustainable levels and impose unfair conditions upon them". This declaration came against the backdrop of protests by farmers against supermarkets across European countries like France, Italy, the Netherlands, Belgium, Ireland and Hungary. The nature of the complaints were similar: the giant retailers were squeezing the prices paid to farmers for products like milk, meat, poultry and wine, in some instances forcing them to sell at below cost prices. In 2010, the US Justice and Agriculture departments also jointly conducted workshops and public hearings on corporate concentration and competition in the domestic food and agriculture markets. Procurement by MNCs, far from solving the problems of farmers, had only worsened their situation.

In 1998, there were riots in Indonesia, directed at the giant foreign retailers who had squeezed out the traditional indigenous retail industry. The impact on the traditional retail trade in Malaysia was so sudden and so adverse that the government had to step in with restrictions (non-tariff barriers). With the aim of "fair and orderly development of the industry", the government introduced a committee on "wholesale and retail trade" and made approval from the committee mandatory for foreign investors. Only one hypermarket is permitted per 350,000 people and no new hypermarket is permitted within 35 km of existing town centres or housing estates.

Given the experience of countries the world over, it is difficult to understand how consumers will benefit from the permitting of MNC retailers to set up shop in India. With their operating mark-ups generally running to many times the retail mark-ups in India, these companies will contribute to higher prices once they have a dominant foothold in the market share. They practice predatory pricing to kill the competition and get a monopolistic position in the retail market. To expect that the consumers will benefit from the entry of MNC retailers is a myth created by transnational retailers.

There is another important aspect that needs to be borne in mind. Transnational retailers employ ruthless methods in the purchase of their products and beat down the prices of their suppliers to unremunerative levels. Walmart imports very large quantities of goods from China (where the government dictates labor policies) and dumps these in their stores in the USA and other countries. In the USA, for instance, this has adversely affected the footwear and hosiery industry, rendering large numbers of workers jobless. Do we want to allow our small/medium scale industries to be harmed in this manner?

The supermarkets form an oligopsony or complex monopsony – that is, they exercise considerable power over suppliers. Hence, they are in a position to dictate prices to their suppliers while retaining their ability to decide on the prices they charge the consumer. Nearly 5 crore people, employed in 1.30 crore small and medium retail stores, earn their livelihoods from this activity. As mentioned by the Parliamentarian Standing Committee, the present set up of retail marketing is most suitable for our conditions. This is evident from Table 7.1 and the fact that in countries that allowed unbridled expansion of MNC retailers, the small, street corner vendors have faced large scale closures.

Table 7.1: List of top countries with organized retail

Country	Current share of organized retailing (%)
USA	80
UK	80
Western European Countries	70
Brazil	40
Thailand	40
Korea	35
India	04

Source: CRISIL & FICCI, 2011

A retail supermarket shrinks the number of intermediaries between the farm and the final consumers, lowering the costs but also taking away jobs. In a country with no social security net, the replacement of lakhs of retailers by a handful of giant intermediaries could result in a shrinking job market. India needs to be extremely careful before a decision is taken on allowing FDI in multi-brand retail. For the present, it appears that the Government of India should roll back its decision to permit FDI in retail. India cannot afford to have large-scale closures of small street corner retailers, as has happened in many other countries. Opposition to FDI in the country's retail sector has also come from an unlikely quarter – Britain, which is the parent country of a few of the MNC retailers looking to enter the Indian market. According to Business Line from July 15th, 2010, a British Member of Parliament (MP) has said that the Indian Government would need to tread "very carefully" if it opened up multi-brand retail to FDI, because the entry of companies like UK-based retailer Tesco would "literally change the fabric of life in India" by endangering small shops.

The government is currently holding consultations on allowing companies such as USA-based Walmart and Tesco to come in. Critics have urged the government to insert safety clauses following protests from small independent retailers that potentially face closure. "Britain was a nation of small shopkeepers, all of that has changed, this is because of supermarkets led by Tesco and it is impossible for small shopkeepers, who have so much to offer, to compete with the prices of supermarkets", stated British MP Amess.

Conclusion

It can be observed from the above analysis that FDI in retail has been a bane to developing countries like India, and this calls for a judicious decision regarding FDI in multi-brand retail. Therefore, it is advisable to frame new rules and regulations in order to regulate the operations of corporates in the retail sector, so the predatory approach of MNCs can be controlled. This will provide other forms of law-abiding organized retailing to grow along with unorganized retailing. The government can try to ensure that domestic and foreign players are on an approximately equal footing and that domestic traders are not at a disadvantage. The small retailers must be given ample opportunity to be able to provide more personalized service so that their higher costs are not affected by the presence of big supermarkets and hypermarkets. Most of the consumers in India, particularly in urban areas, are exposed to the benefits and experience of the organized form of retail. It will be difficult to deny the same benefits and experience to consumers in other areas for a very long period. India is a big and growing market. Both unorganized and FDI-led retail sectors need to co-exist. Policy makers must ensure a level playing field for small retailers. The availability of better credit facilities to unorganized retailers, from banks and micro-finance institutions, would enable them to be more competitive. There should be a gradual opening of the retail sector to provide the domestic industry with enough time to adjust to the changes.

References

Asian Development Bank. 2004. "Asian Development Outlook 2004". *Part 3: Foreign Direct Investment in Developing Asia*. Manila: Asian Development Bank.

Arabi, Urmi. 2005. "Foreign Direct Investment (FDI's) Flows and sustained growth: A case study of India and China". *Dynamics,*

Economic Growth, and International Trade in its series DEGIT Conference Papers. New Delhi: DEGIT. Accessed February 7, 2014 http://www.degit.ifw-kiel.de/papers/degit_10/C010_044.pdf.

Audit Committee Institute. 2010. "FDI in Multi-Brand Retail Trading". Mumbai, KPMG. Accessed March 11, 2014 https://www.in.kpmg.com/SecureData/ACI/Files/FDI_in_retail2.pdf.

CRISIL. 2012. "CRISIL opinion". Mumbai: CRISIL Limited. Accessed January 23, 2014 http://www.crisil.com/pdf/research/CRISIL-Research-indian retail_sep12.pdf.

Department of Industrial Policy & Promotion. 2007. *Fact Sheet on Foreign Direct Investment. Ministry of Commerce and Industry*, New Delhi, Accessed December 11, 2013 (http://dipp.gov.in/fdi_statistics/india_fdi_jan_2007.pdf).

FICCI. 2012. 'Impact of FDI in Retail on Stakeholders'. New Delhi: FICCI. Accessed January 17, 2014 http://www.ficci.com/spdocument/20181/FICCIReport%20onFDIinRetail.pdf.

Economic Survey (2011-12). 2012. New Delhi: Government of India. Accessed August 11, 2013. http://indiabudget.nic.in/es2011-12/estat1.pdf.

PRS Legislative Research Report. 2009. "Nineteenth report on Foreign and Domestic investment in Retail Sector". New Delhi: PRS Legislative Research. Accessed June 4, 2014 http://www.prsindia.org/uploads/media/vikas_doc/docs/1244460168~~Foreign%20&%20Domestic%20Investment%20in%20Retail%20Sector.pdf.

Retail Practice. 2008, 'The Great Indian Bazaar: Organised Retail Comes of Age in India'. Mumbai: McKinsey & Company.

Shepherd, Andrew. 2004. "The implications of supermarket development for horticultural farmers and traditional marketing systems in Asia", *paper presented at FAO/AFMA/FAMA Regional Workshop on The Growth of Supermarkets as Retailers of Fresh Produce*, Kuala Lumpur, October 4-7, 2004, Accessed April 19, 2014 http://www.fao.org/ag/ags/subjects/en/agmarket/docs/asia_sups.pdf.

Technopak Projections. 1999. "Changing Retail Landscape". Accessed November 27, 2013, www.ksa-technopak.com

The Economic Times Bureau. 2010. "BJP opposes FDI in multi-brand retail." *The Economic Times*, July 8. Accessed October 22, 2013 http://economictimes.indiatimes.com/news/politics/nation/BJP-opposes-FDI-in-multibrand- retail/articleshow/6140941.cms.

CHAPTER EIGHT

THE BUSINESS PROCESS MANAGEMENT INDUSTRY IN INDIA: REVIEWING ITS NATURE, SIZE AND DIRECTION

HASTIMAL G. SAGARA

Introduction

India is at the forefront of the rapidly evolving global IT-Business Process Outsourcing (BPO), now known as Business Process Management, market and is well established as a 'destination of choice'. Today, superlatives such as, for instance, 'soft superpower', 'IT hub' and 'world's IT-Capital' have become synonymous with India for its Information Technology (IT) industry, which worth over USD 100 billion and is responsible for two thirds of the world's total exports of software. It provides direct employment to about 2.8 million and indirect employment to 8.9 million people.

This paper is an attempt to explore and study the emergence and transformation of the Information Technology sector and to map the policy initiatives related to the IT sector in the post-reform period, in India in general and Gujarat in particular. The paper identifies complex issues related to work and workers, revenue, exports, etc., in the computer hardware, software services and IT-BPO sector in Gujarat. Factors responsible for the uneven regional distribution of the software services and IT-BPO industry are also discussed here. Further, the study enquires into the processes explaining the unimpressive performance of the state of Gujarat in this sector, particularly as compared to the southern Indian states. It tries to estimate the impact of the current global recession on the foreign demand driven software services and ITeS industry in India in general and the state of Gujarat in particular.

Objectives of the Study

1. To map the policy initiatives of governments towards rendering the IT industry competitive, both at the national and the state level, during the period of economic reforms
2. To find out the nature and composition of IT/ITeS firms in Gujarat and to identify factors affecting the IT/ITeS sector in the state
3. To estimate the growth and transformation of the computer software services and IT-BPO sector in India in general and Gujarat in particular
4. To analyse issues concerning earnings, social security benefits, labour attrition, training, career opportunities in the IT/ITeS sector, etc. in Gujarat
5. To discuss future challenges to the software services and IT-BPO sector, in India in general and Gujarat in particular

Review of Literature

According to the 2011-12 Annual Report of the Department of Electronics and Information Technology, Ministry of Communication and Information Technology, Government of India, "2011-12 was a landmark year for the IT-BPO industry in India crossing the USD 100 billion mark. IT services still account for a dominant share of IT-BPO exports". Pradhan and Abraham (2005) concluded that as many as 400 of the *Fortune 500* companies either have their own centres in India or are currently outsourcing work to Indian firms. This clearly shows that India enjoys a very dominant position in IT-BPO exports.

Indian firms operate not only at the low end of the IT-BPO industry; they are increasingly expanding their businesses into higher value IT software development and ITeS. According to the 2011-12 Annual Report of the National Association of Software Services Companies (NASSCOM), the Global Knowledge Process Outsourcing (KPO) Services segment was only a negligible part of the IT and ITeS industry 10 years ago, but today, India's KPO industry earns around 70 per cent of the global revenues of this industry, employs an estimated 70,000 people, and has been growing at around 24 per cent annually over the past five years. It is now emerging as a full-fledged industry in the country. KPO has tremendous potential that India could explore through a favourable policy to create employment opportunities for experts in areas such as law, education, health, etc.

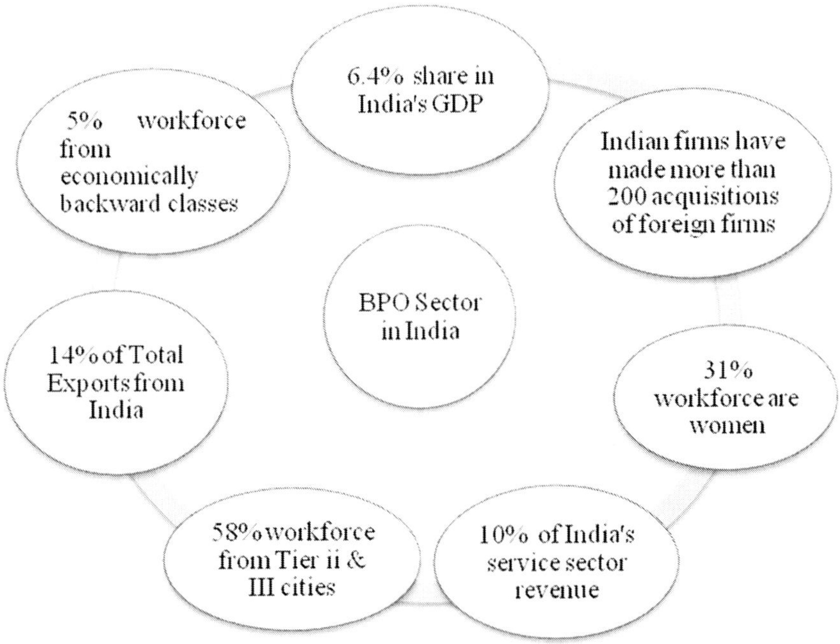

Sources: NASSCOM as on January 21 (2014)

Figure 8.1: IT-BPO Sector in India

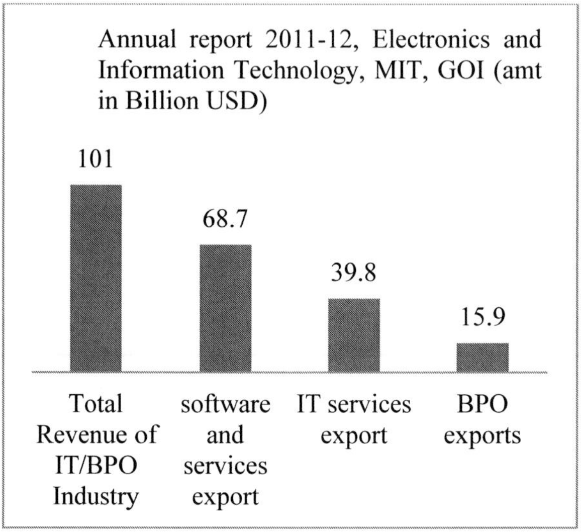

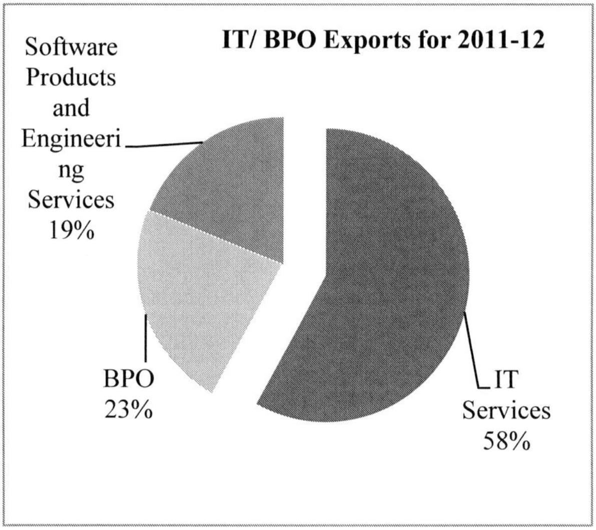

Source: Ministry of Information and Communication Technology

Figure 8.2: IT-BPO Services Revenues and Exports (2011-12)

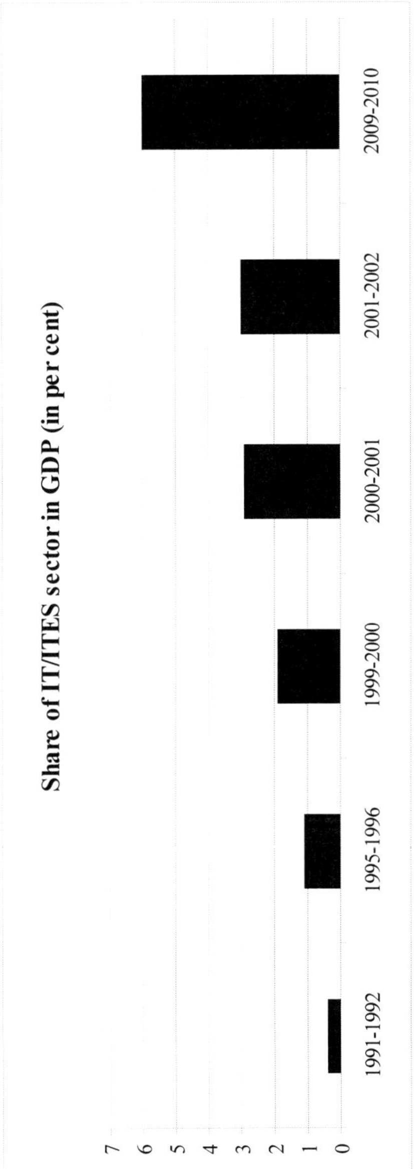

Source: Dataquest for IT Industry Output

Figure 8.3: Share of IT/ITeS Sector in GDP for Various Years

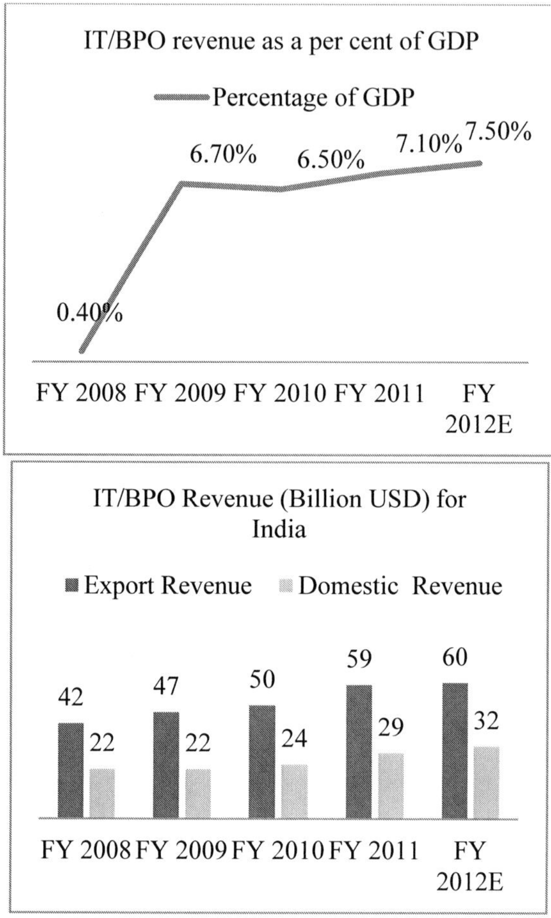

Source: NASSCOM

Figure 8.4: Revenue of IT/ITeS Sector

According to NASSCOM, 2012 was a milestone year for the Indian IT-BPO industry – aggregate revenues crossed the USD 100 billion mark and exports stood at USD 69 billion. Within the global sourcing industry, India was able to increase its market share from 51 per cent in 2009 to 58 per cent in 2011, highlighting India's continued competitiveness and the effectiveness of India-based providers delivering transformational benefits. Export revenues (including hardware) are estimated have touched USD 69.1 billion in FY2012, increasing by over 16 per cent compared to the previous year, while domestic revenues (including hardware) amounted to about USD 31.7 billion, growing by over 9 per cent. Software and services revenues (excluding hardware), comprising nearly 87 per cent of total industry revenues, were estimated at USD 87.6 billion in FY2012 – a growth of about 14.9 per cent over FY2011. Within software and services exports, IT services account for 58 per cent, BPO for nearly 23 per cent and ER&D and software products for 19 per cent. The industry continues to be a net employment generator, with an estimated 230,000 jobs created in FY2012, providing direct employment to about 2.8 million, and indirectly employing 8.9 million people. As a proportion of national GDP, sector revenues have grown from 1.2 per cent in FY1998 to an estimated 7.5 per cent in FY2012. The industry's share in total Indian exports (merchandise plus services) increased from less than 4 per cent in FY1998 to about 25 per cent in FY2012.

India has a vast workforce of young, college-going, urban, educated, English-speaking, tech-savvy people, which is readily available to work in the IT industry. Indian costs are roughly one third of the global cost of similar services and efficiency is on par with international standards. These factors have catalysed India's progress in the software services and ITeS industry. Companies from the US and the EU outsource business to save time, cost and resources. However, the Indian IT/ITeS sector faces major challenges from prominent global competitors, including China, the Philippines and Costa Rica.

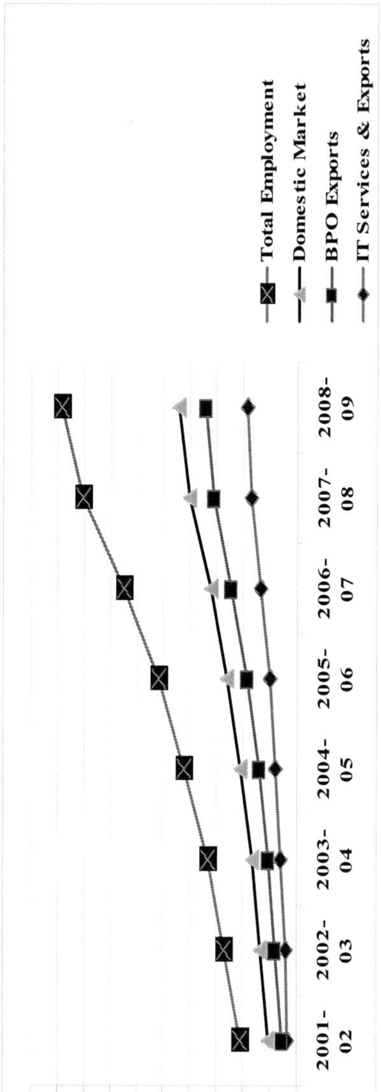

Source: Ministry of Information and Communication Technology

Figure 8.5: Employment in India (in millions)

According to task fragmentation theory, activities in the software production process are divided into conception and execution tasks. Conception tasks involve preliminary analysis and the designing of software and conception workers perform high-skill activities as project managers and project leaders. The execution tasks involve coding, testing, maintenance, etc., and execution workers perform low-skill activities as developers, module leaders, etc. The low-level workers have limited career growth opportunities, which deprive them of opportunities to upgrade their skills, and they experience only horizontal movement or virtual promotions (Ilavarasan 2008).

Evidence on the link between skill upgrades and worker stability suggests that skill upgrade policy may have a role to play in creating greater employee stability in software firms. Abundant lifelong learning opportunities at low cost may keep attrition rates lower. Similarly, standardised pay packages across the industry and skill levels may reduce attrition. Reducing the attrition rate is very important to control the spiralling efficiency wage for workers which, in turn, would keep the software industry internationally competitive (Abraham 2007).

The Indian IT industry is often represented as providing employment opportunities to a wider cross section of society than has been the case with other professional and white-collar jobs. However, available data suggest that the social composition of the IT workforce is more homogeneous than is often supposed, in that the workforce is largely urban, middle/upper class, and high/middle caste. The process of exclusion that operates in the educational system and in recruitment, as well as the ideology of 'merit' in the context of elite opposition to reservation, create this relative social homogeneity in the IT workforce (Upadhya 2007).

The business of outsourcing is largely dominated by the South Asian region in general and India in particular. The rankings, according to the Tholons' Annual Reports for 2013 and 2014, show eight cities from Asia standing among the top 10. According to the same reports, four out of the five top outsourcing cities are in India. The Philippines is fast catching up, with two cities, Manila and Cebu, ranking second and ninth in the list of top ten BPO destinations. The southern Indian cities, i.e. Bengaluru, Chennai, Hyderabad and Mumbai, dominate the business (Table 8.1).

Table 8.1: Tholons Top 100 Outsourcing Destinations: Ranking for 2013 and 2014

Country	City	Rank in 2014	Rank in 2013
India	Bangalore	1	1
Philippines	Manila (NCR)	2	3
India	Mumbai	3	2
India	Delhi (NCR)	4	4
India	Chennai	5	5
India	Hyderabad	6	6
India	Pune	7	7
Philippines	Cebu City	8	8
Poland	Kraków	9	10
Ireland	Dublin	10	9

Source: www.tholons.com

IT and the Role of Government in India

State policies in the 1980s acknowledged for the first time the importance of software development and underlined the need for institutional and policy support. A policy shift that allowed greater play to market forces, a gradual reduction in government controls and a larger role for the private sector began in 1986. An explicit software policy was announced, underlining the importance of the integrated development of the software industry for the domestic and export markets and providing greater incentives, such as tax holidays, tax exemption on income from software exports, export subsidies, and duty-free import of hardware and software, for the industry to grow.

With the economic reforms that began in 1991, a number of other policy initiatives facilitated the growth of IT. A new policy included the provision to finance software development through equity and venture capital, measures to make available faster and cheaper data communication facilities, the removal of entry barriers for foreign companies and a reduction and rationalisation of taxes, duties and tariffs. But it was the creation of a series of software technology parks under the aegis of the Software Technology Park of India (STPI) that revolutionised the development of the software industry, leading to the mushrooming of several local IT companies (Taganas and Kaul 2006). The Government of India formulated a national IT policy in 1998 and set up a National Task Force on Information Technology and Software Development, which aimed to make India an 'IT superpower'.

It is clear that Indian IT/ITeS has grown in leaps and bounds, for various reasons. But the most important factor has been the positive role played by the Government of India and the governments of some states like Karnataka, Tamil Nadu, Andhra Pradesh, Maharashtra, etc. The millennium bug, famously known as Y2K, that could have jeopardised the working of computers in the present century, cheaper labour in India, conducive economic reforms, etc., are some of the other factors that facilitated the growth of the IT/ITeS sector in India.

Labour Issues in the IT Industry

The call centres in Bangalore city are housed in multi-purpose buildings, such as the gleaming International Tech Park (ITPL), complete with a granite façade waterfall, gym, coffee shop and restaurants, and the modern look and feel of the call centres stands in stark contrast to the surrounding semi-urban villages and slums (McMillin 2006). The superior work environment, use of state-of-the-art technology in day-to-day work, better salary structure, catchy designations, smart, young peer workers etc. tend to make workers believe that the job being carried out is that of an executive or professional (Remesh 2004).

Organisations in the ITeS sector have been extremely successful in keeping unions at bay. They adopt strategies reinforcing the notion of corporate culturalism, which aims at winning the ‘hearts and minds’ of employees by managing what they think and feel, and not just how they behave (Noronha and D’Cruz 2006). According to Remesh (2004): “Employment in the IT industry implies a host of insecurities and vulnerability, which is partially reflected in the high attrition rate. The work is too demanding, depressing and demeaning. Most of these youngsters are in fact burning out their formative years. The other blatant insecurity is the complete absence of organizational activities, as the philosophy of work organization is based on individualization. The young employees represent a group of expensively educated cheap labour and the long-term opportunity cost in terms of working in IT industry with total insecurity could be very high.”

Research Methodology

In order to make this piece of research more comprehensive and inclusive, both primary and secondary data were used. Primary data were collected through fieldwork with the help of a predetermined set of questionnaires and focus group discussions to complement the secondary data for a thorough research study.

Although secondary data relate mostly to the reform period, data have been collected from 1991 onwards from India/Gujarat. Data from grey data sources like newspapers and magazines were also used. Newspaper clippings of recruitment advertisements were taken from the *Times of India*, Ahmedabad, and *Divya Bhaskar*, Ahmedabad, for the first half of 2012, and used to identify the nature, terms and conditions of recruitment by the IT-BPO firms in Ahmedabad.

Secondary data were collected from available policy documents/reports, the annual reports of relevant ministries, both at the central and state levels, and NASSCOM, Dataquest and other databases. Statistical tools like histograms, trend lines, etc. have been used to show significant changes in economic variables.

The primary data were collected with the help of a field survey through an unstructured set of questions posed to about 25 young BPO employees and five managerial level people/employers who have hands on experience with the ITeS sector – call centres, BPOs, KPOs, etc. – in Ahmedabad. The stratified random sampling method was used in order to include all types of call centres, such as inbound/outbound, domestic/international, voice-based/non-voice-based etc. A 'focus group discussion' was also conducted among four employees of an international call centre, as a research tool to collect data from stakeholders. The aim was to collect both quantitative and qualitative data from these stakeholders.

The field survey and focus group discussion broadly included the following variables/aspects related to the labour force in the IT sector in Gujarat: the nature and terms of employment of workers; socio-economic and demographic profiles of employees; the recruitment and training process; problems of labour attrition and work environment; health related problems with labour, social security and other benefits for employees, and gender specific issues.

Research Findings and Conclusions

From the graph below, it is evident that Bengaluru, with 315 firms, still leads other cities in the country in terms of the number of firms registered with NASSCOM, distantly followed by Mumbai and Chennai, with 206 and 184 respectively. Ahmedabad has just 34 registered firms; this shows that Gujarat in general and Ahmedabad in particular have not been among the first choices of destination for IT/ITeS business in India. The first 10 cities account for more than three quarters of the total number of firms registered with NASSCOM. Southern Indian cities have almost half the share.

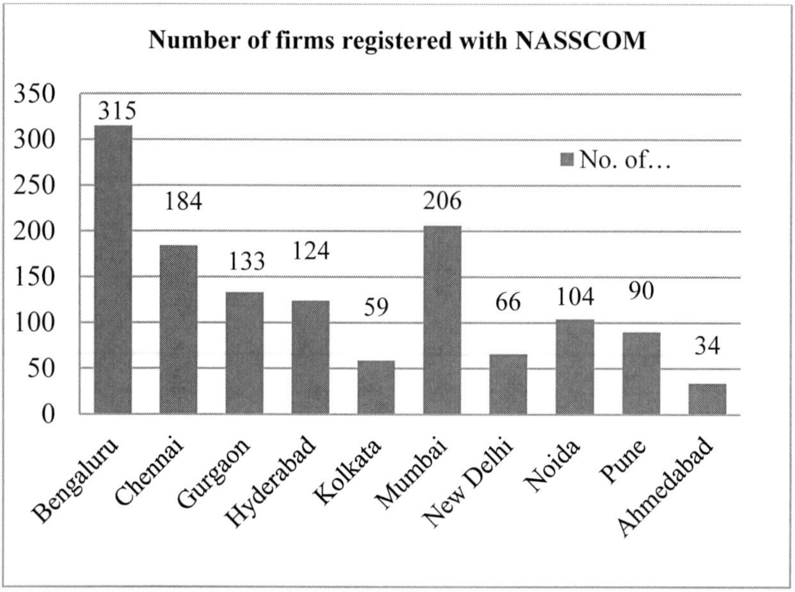

Source: NASSCOM

Figure 8.6: No. of firms registered with NASSCOM as of Jan 27, 2013

IT-BPO Industry in Gujarat

From this research study, it has become clear that Gujarat has lagged behind the southern states in terms of number of people employed, output, profits and revenues in the IT/ITeS sector. The outsourcing business in Gujarat is principally concentrated in the cities of Gandhinagar, Ahmedabad and Vadodara and is thinly spread in Surat, Rajkot, Bhuj and other places. The major concentration of the BPO industry is in the newly developed areas of Ahmedabad and Vadodara, and the SEZ area of Gandhinagar. There are about 1,400 IT/ITeS companies, with a turnover of USD 1 billion, in Gujarat (Indian Express 2014).

The IT-SEZ Infocity is the major IT hub in Gandhinagar. And with the completion of the upcoming GIFT (Gujarat International Finance Tech) City in Gandhinagar in less than half a decade, the IT sector in the state is likely to get a shot in the arm in the coming years. Ahmedabad is increasingly becoming an IT centre for web designing and hosting, mobile applications and solutions, cloud computing, gaming, and Wi-Fi technology, to meet local demand. The clientele for small-sized IT firms in

Ahmedabad range from educational institutes to small and medium enterprises within Gujarat. These firms are largely promoted by young entrepreneurs and they provide all kinds of IT services.

Gujarat IT firms have relatively good local demand, for both hardware and software products. Although manufacturing of hardware does not take place in Gujarat, trading, particularly in retail, is proving to be big business and Ahmedabad has become an alternative market to buy IT products, particularly for buyers from neighbouring states who do not like the Mumbai and Delhi markets.

Ahmedabad has all kinds of BPO firms – inbound and outbound, domestic and international, voice-based and non-voice-based, debt collection etc. Voice-based call centres constitute the bulk of the BPO industry in Ahmedabad. Domestic IT/ITeS firms operate in areas like telecommunications and DTH TV channels services in Rajasthan, Gujarat, and Madhya Pradesh. International call centres operate in billing, accounting, consultancy, education/auto loans, medical consultancies, debt collection, etc. for clientele based in the US (major outsourcers to IT/ITeS firms in Ahmedabad), the UK, Australia, Canada, Germany etc.

There are two categories of BPO firms or call centres in Gujarat: large firms, which operate on several outsourcing projects at a time, and small ones, which deal with one or two contracts at a time. Ahmedabad has over a decade-old, large-sized BPO firms such as MOTIF, AEGIS, AZURE, AXIOM etc. However, small-sized call centres outnumber the bigger ones. Large firms (with over 100 employees) get IT/ITeS projects that are bigger in size, longer in duration and are from companies; smaller firms find it far more difficult to sustain themselves – they appear and disappear depending upon the availability of projects, employees and financial resources. The clientele is largely from the West. Small IT firms take on very limited and time-bound outsourcing projects compared to the larger ones, which work with MNCs from the West.

There are both domestic and international call centres in Ahmedabad, Gandhinagar and Baroda, but the number of the former is quite negligible compared to the latter. Large firms provide IT/ITeS services both within and outside the country, but the smaller ones manage to get only international, time-bound projects related to voice- and non-voice-based assignments.

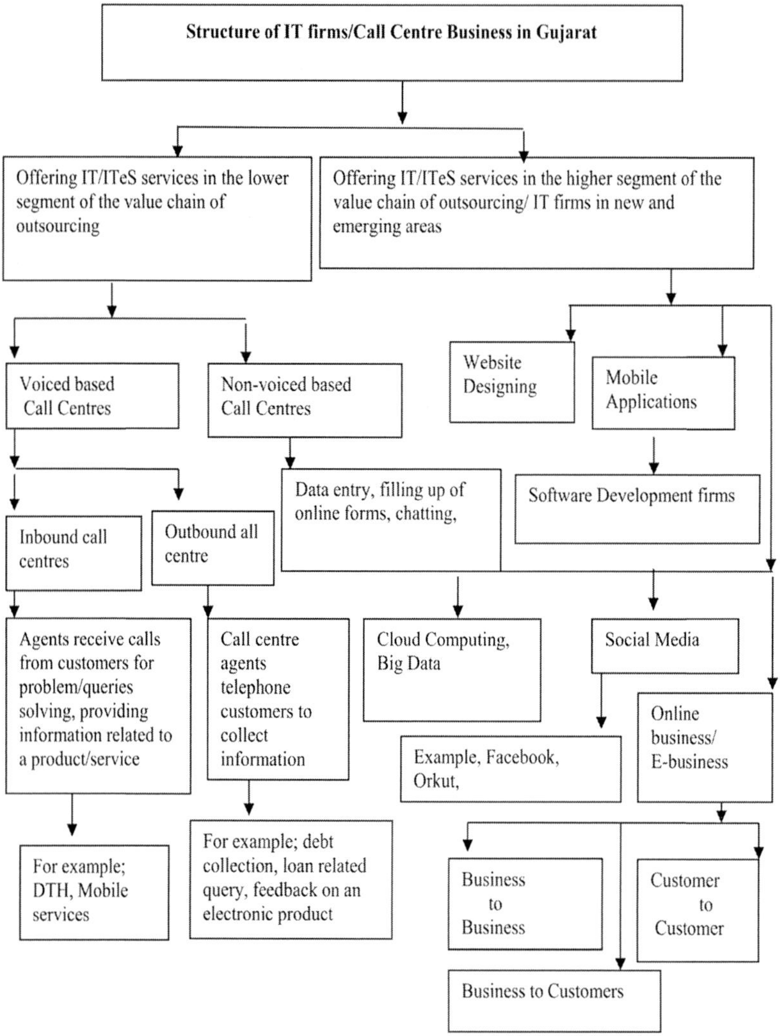

Source: Prepared by the author

Figure 8.7: Structure of IT Firms/Call Centre Businesses in Gujarat

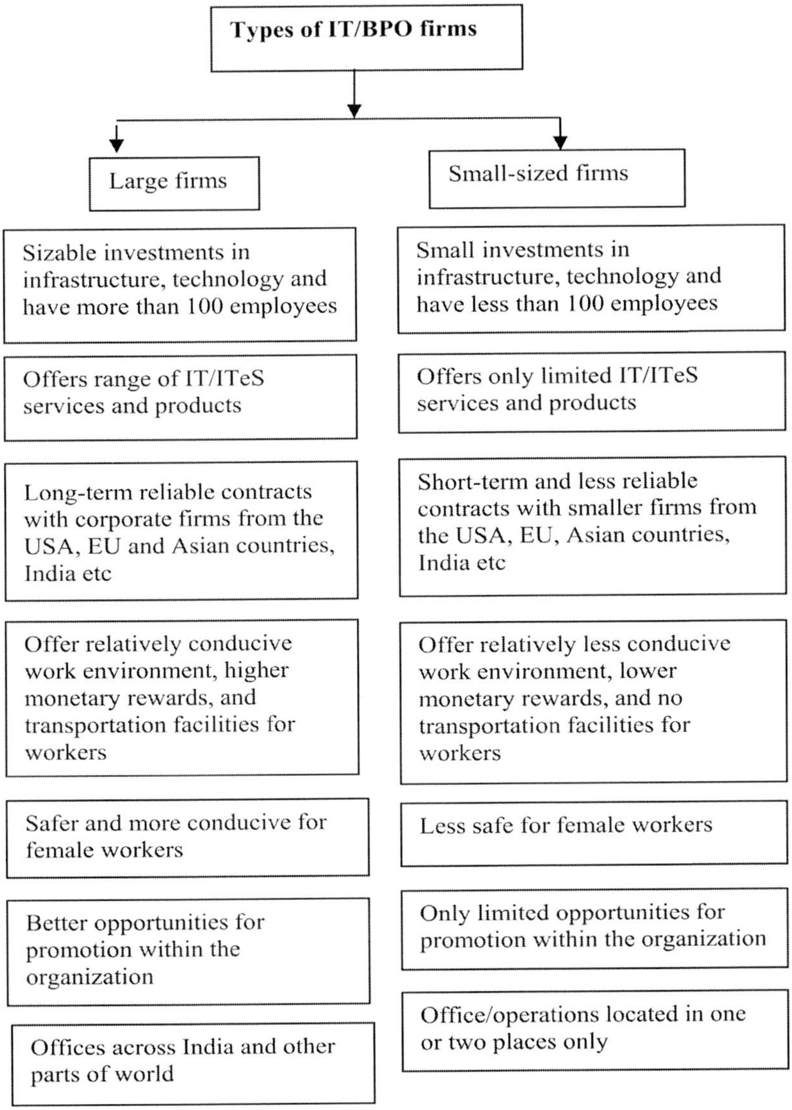

Source: Field survey by the author

Figure 8.8: Types of BPO Firms in Ahmedabad

Types of IT-BPO Firms

The most remarkable aspect of IT-BPO firms in Gujarat is their ability to adapt to new outsourcing processes or technology. IT/ITeS firms in Gujarat explore all kinds of clients all over to get contracts – big or small – for any type of outsourcing process, regardless of whether they have served in a similar field in the past. Therefore, the IT-BPO firms in Gujarat always show a readiness to offer their clients all kinds of IT-enabled services, ranging from low end 'data entry work' to high value software development and knowledge process outsourcing.

Large IT-BPO firms, like MOTIF, AEGIG, AZURE, GATEWAY Technolabs, Diamond Infosystems, etc., with their head/corporate offices in Gujarat are not confined in their operations to that state alone, but have offices and operations spread between major cities all over the country, as well as across the world. For example, MOTIF has offices not only in Ahmedabad and Delhi in India, but also in California in the US, Manila in the Philippines and Sane Jose in Costa Rica. The logic behind having branches all over the world is for managing varied types of process. However, small firms with limited investment and few employees operate from one or two places only. The large firms also have the ability and resources to use both their human and technological expertise across their centres of operations. This implies that whenever the need arises, people with certain technological expertise from one place are shifted to another by the company to take care of a process or a project there.

Employment and Work Conditions

The BPO firms in Ahmedabad, Gandhinagar and Baroda recruit principally urban, convent educated, unmarried boys and girls with good communication skills at entry level. Recruitment is a continuous process involving advertising in both English and vernacular newspapers and/or on internet job sites. In order to attract a larger number of applicants, IT recruiters post advertisements for the recruitment of hundreds of call centre agents, although they actually need far fewer. But the biggest intake of employees is done through job placement agencies and the personal contacts of employees, who are made lucrative offers and given incentives to bring in new employees. For corporate type BPOs/call centres, a candidate's interview may run on for several days before he/she is finalised. Small-sized call centres recruit agents with less formality and screening compared to their larger counterparts. Corporate houses, for their BPO businesses, are very particular in ascertaining the fulfilment of minimum standards, formalities and the educational qualifications of the applicants during the process of recruitment, but the smaller ones are less rigid and recruit agents just on the basis of good communication skills. A new recruit in a large call centre starts regular work only after undergoing 15 days or more of in-house training led by the senior cadre of employees or trainers.

Source: Field survey by author

Figure 8.9: IT-BPO Sector Organisation Hierarchy

Each BPO firm in Gujarat has two major departments, namely an operations department and a quality audit and training department. The operations department consists of call centre agents, their coach and team leaders and the managers. The quality control or audit department, relatively smaller in size, takes care of auditing calls by agents in terms of number of calls attended to per unit of time, discipline, communication skills, convincing power etc. The cadre of employees in the processes of a large BPO firm goes by and large in the following order: call centre representative, team coach, team leader, assistant manager, manager, vice president, president, CEO/CFO etc. The lower levels of the hierarchy are revenue generators and are large in number compared to the management level employees.

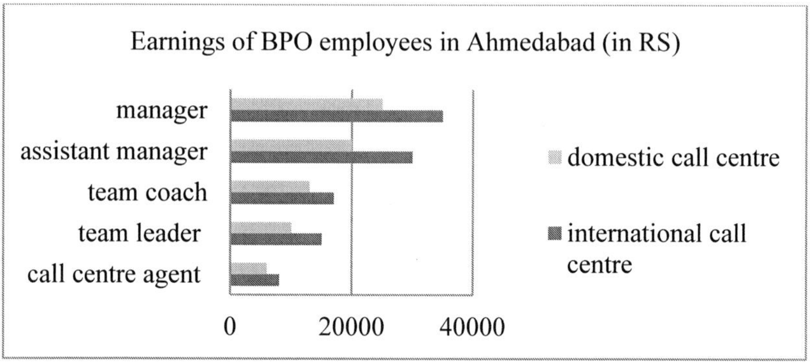

Source: Calculated on the basis of field survey by author

Figure 8.10: Earnings of BPO Employees in Ahmedabad (in Rs)

Salaries in Ahmedabad-based BPOs depend upon the nature and size of the call centre, as well as the experience of the agents in the call centre. International BPO firms, for which command of English language is a prerequisite, offer starting salaries as high as Rs 10,000 per month, but domestic ones pay only around Rs 6,000 per month. Team leaders and managerial positions draw salaries that are as much as 30 and 50 per cent higher than the entry level agents. Jumping from one firm to another helps an agent earn more. Any call centre agent can learn the complete process in the span of two months or less and apply for a job at a higher salary based on that experience. The opportunity to increase their earnings is better for agents who leave one firm for another compared to the ones who stick with one company for a long time. Vertical rises or promotions and greater responsibilities are available to older employees of the organisation.

Composition of IT-BPO Employees

Most BPO workers are either high school leavers or mere graduates. Not even a single entry level call centre representative is an engineer, has an MBA, CA or CS or possesses any other reputed professional degree in BPO firms in Ahmedabad. Both genders are fairly represented here. The IT/ITeS workforce, while principally being from Gujarat, also comprises people from Rajasthan, Maharashtra and Madhya Pradesh. The percentage of the SC/ST community is below five per cent of the total workforce in international call centres, but it is twice as much in their domestic counterparts. There is no caste discrimination experienced by employees from underprivileged communities in the IT-BPO industry in Ahmedabad or in other cities of Gujarat.

IT/ITeS firms that operate in areas such as software development, web designing, cloud computing, mobile applications, etc. mostly recruit people who have either similar academic backgrounds or hands-on experience in the area. Applicants with non-technical backgrounds are generally not considered. The proportion of female and SC/ST employees is less than a quarter in such purely IT-based technical jobs.

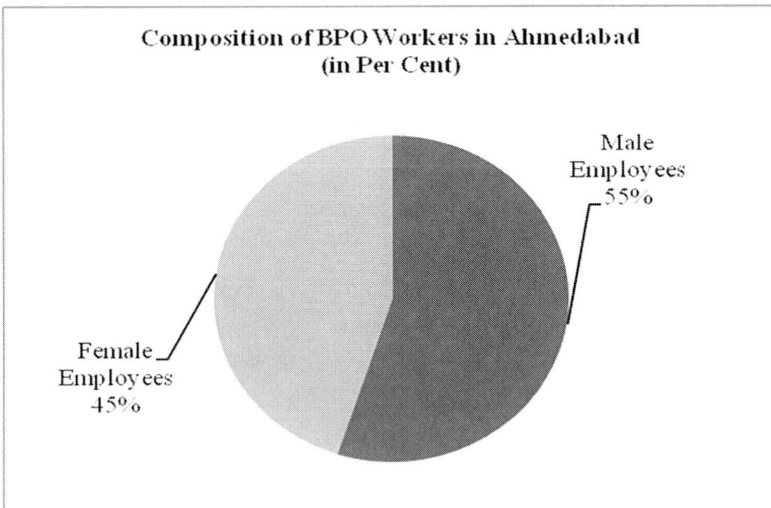

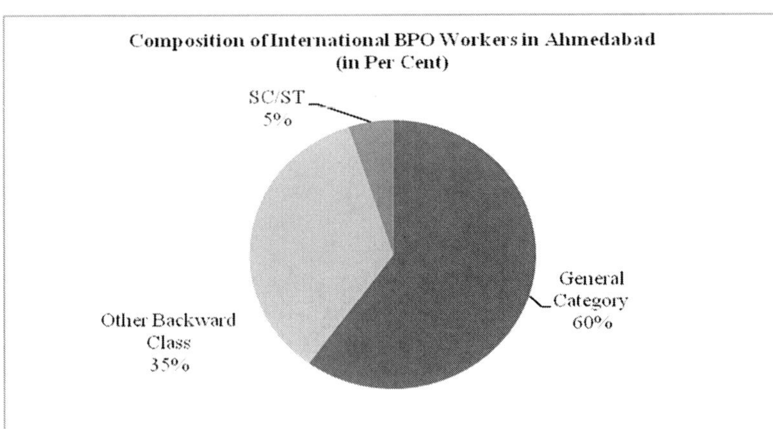

Source: Estimates from the field survey by author

Figure 8.11: Composition of International BPO Workers in Ahmedabad

Social and Economic Security of the Employees and Attrition

Small-sized call centres do not provide the type of benefits to their employees that are available to the workforce in the organised sector. Corporate type BPO firms provide certain benefits like provident funds, weeks off, leave and performance-based incentives. Drop off and pick up facilities are made available for night shift workers. Recreation, free food, cafeteria facilities, etc. are available only in a selected few firms. Female employees have separate washrooms/toilets at the workplace in large corporate BPO firms. An agent may lose his/her job due to uninformed and frequent leave, misbehaviour with clients over the phone, lack of professionalism in the workplace, etc. No entry level employees wish to stay at a call centre for their lifelong careers; the managerial cadre workers, however, find it a lucrative career option for its earnings, challenges and learning.

Workers are in demand when an ITeS firm is awarded a project, but they are laid off during lean business periods. The stakeholders rightly say that neither the employees nor the BPO firms themselves are permanent in nature.

The entrepreneurs in the IT/ITeS sector in Gujarat are young risk takers who have worked in a call centre or BPO firm in the past for a few years and want to set up their own firms.

There are increments and incentives for meeting targets, in the case of telemarketing call centres. The work environment in corporate type call centres is reasonably conducive and generally liked by employees as compared to their smaller counterparts, where exploitation of workers persists extensively.

Employee turnover is a major concern for call centres in Gujarat too. The attrition rate among employees in the lower segment is in the range of 15-30 per cent. Competition among firms to recruit and retain good BPO workers is fierce. Workers are lured by promises of better salaries, attractive perks, incentives, promotions, free board and lodging etc.

Like other states, the process of informalisation is visible in the BPO sector of Gujarat. Globalisation has brought in flexible labour laws, difficulty in forming trade unions for workers and the absence of social security benefits for employees in the long run.

Therefore, there is job dissatisfaction, and so, the attrition rate in BPOs is around 25 per cent on an annual basis. Workers frequently switch over to other firms for better pay and perks, promotions, and work environments. The opportunities to progress vertically for an employee within a firm are few, although monetary rewards continually rise. No one joins this sector to work on a permanent basis; it is a make-shift arrangement for those who want to earn handsomely while studying or until they get alternative employment.

There are health related and other concerns among the IT/ITeS workers, like loss of sleep and appetite, indigestion, depression, break up of friendships/social circles etc.

Important reasons for the high attrition rate in the BPO industry in Ahmedabad:

1. Lack of a conducive work environment in present assignment with a call centre
2. Higher monetary rewards offered elsewhere in factories/offices
3. Job content does not improve biodata or profile
4. Inflexible and tight work schedules
5. Severe mental stress and other health problems

Important reasons for employees sticking with the IT/ITeS industry are:

1. Non-availability of job opportunities in other sectors
2. Poor educational qualifications or technical or professional degrees at an early age
3. Lack of technical skills or other professional expertise required for other industries
4. Modern work environment and young and energetic colleagues
5. Easy money and perks and incentives that become handy for day-to-day expenses

It is not always the employee alone who is responsible for leaving a BPO job. The processes/projects of IT/ITeS firms are time-bound. Employment lasts as long as the project does. One major excuse given by employers to employees for the latter's termination is the poor quality in handling calls by agents. The quality control (QC) department of each BPO firm maintains a record of 'how effectively an agent handles a call'. Employers use the excuse of sub-standard performance or misbehaviour by the agent, as per the QC records, to lay off workers. Generally, BPO firms terminate employees in the months of December and January every year when IT-BPO demand is low in western countries. Too many or too frequent unpermitted absences from work can also result in employees losing their jobs. However, some of the star performers as per QC records are retained by firms.

Web Designing: a Leading IT Process in Ahmedabad

According to the Tholons Report of December 2013, "Ahmedabad stands at 63rd position in the Top 100 outsourcing destinations in the world". An increasing number of Ahmedabad-based IT firms are taking up web design, animation and multimedia, and mobile application development as their core activities. One can find such firms spread all across the major cities of Gujarat, particularly Ahmedabad, Baroda, and Gandhinagar. The demand for such IT services is mostly local. From newspaper advertisement clippings, it is clear that IT firms in Ahmedabad are in constant need of employees trained in web design, Android, iPad and Titanium Development, HTML 5 Programming, PHP Programming, Wordpress Technology etc. This kind of ITeS technology, commonly called IT solutions, is exported to the US, Australia, the UK, etc. Levels of expertise, salaries, working conditions and chances of promotion for employees are higher in these firms compared to the call centres of IT-BPO firms. Web developers and PHP programmers are able to take up independent consultancies, web support assignments and personal individual projects. The demand by local firms for web design is largely unmet, so there is much scope to grow in this type of business.

The IT Sector in Gujarat and the Role of Government

Some state governments have been proactive in boosting the development of the IT sector, like those of Karnataka, Andhra Pradesh, Tamil Nadu, and Maharashtra. These governments have initiated reforms ranging from tax exemptions to labour laws to venture capital for firms in the IT/ITeS sector. Although late, the reforms by the government have been extremely positive and have been instrumental in facilitating the IT-BPO sector to the level it is at today.

Gujarat Electronics and Software Industries Association (GESIA) was formed in Gujarat in 1995 to bring the state up to par with the southern states of India in Information and Communication Technology. It is a not-for-profit, industry-led and industry-managed association of firms offering IT-BPO services. After a decade, GESIA has become the only nodal representative association for the information and communication technology industry in Gujarat, with more than 370 members from various parts of Gujarat. GESIA works in partnership with the Government of Gujarat for the promotion of the software, BPO/KPO, telecom/ISP and electronics industry in the state.

As a state level body, it provides a recognised platform for discussions of and solutions to common issues, as well as for networking amongst its members, professionals and government officials. Over the years, GESIA has formed various partnerships with national level industry associations such as MAIT, NASSCOM, etc., to work with them as their partner in Gujarat. The Government of Gujarat declared a comprehensive and innovative IT Policy in 2006-2011. The salient features of this policy are the following:

- The state government will initiate steps to enhance the supply of skilled manpower for IT/ITeS, such as industry-institute partnerships to enhance industry relevant skills by optimally using existing educational infrastructure, including distance learning through satellite communication facilities available at Bhaskaracharaya Institute for Space Application and Geo-informatics (BISAG).
- The state government will collaborate with NASSCOM to conduct NAC tests for facilitating benchmarking of BPO manpower.
- It will promote mega IT projects on a case-by-case basis, as well as promoting IT parks/SEZs to enhance the availability of ready, built-up space for the IT/ITeS sector.
- The state has provided the facility of self-certification under labour laws. In addition to the relaxation of labour laws, Gujarat's SEZ law provides a host of exemptions from state specific taxes and cesses etc.
- The state government has already set up a Gujarat IT venture fund under the aegis of Gujarat Venture Finance Ltd., Ahmedabad.
- All new information technology industry units have been exempted from the payment of electricity duty for a period of five years from the date on which the unit commences commercial operation.
- Captive power units set up by eligible IT/New IT and ITeS units will be exempted from payment of electricity duty according to the provisions of Section 3 of the Bombay Electricity Duty Act, 1958. IT and ITeS units will be considered eligible for exemption from power cuts.
- In order to facilitate the adequate availability of floor space to IT/ITeS units in urban centres, the government will permit more than the permissible Floor Space Index (FSI) to IT parks, subject to the payment of a premium for the additional FSI at market rates.
- Gujarat Informatics Ltd. has been identified as the nodal agency for the promotion of IT in the state.

- The Government of Gujarat has started many IT-related programmes, such as Gujarat State Wide Area Network (GSWAN), State Wide Attention on Grievances through Application of Technology (SWAGAT Online), e-gram – Vishvagram, *e-city, e-Dhara,* Hospital Management Information System, Integrated Workflow and Document Management System (IWDMS), e-Procurement, Sachivalya Integrated Communication Network (SICN), Information and Communication Technology and e-readiness initiatives, the Gujarat State Data Centre, etc. All these initiatives have made Gujarat one of the leading states in e-governance.

Software Technology Parks and Exports from Gujarat

The most remarkable policy initiative by the Government of India has been the Software Technology Parks of India Act (STPI Act) and the STPI policy. It aims at increasing the production of IT software and ITeS and increasing export of the same, facilitated by the government through fiscal and other concessions. 51 STPI parks have been set up in the country, including Gujarat (Software Technology Parks of Gujarat are listed in Appendix 8.1). More than three quarters of India's software exports to the US and the EU are from the STPI zones. The leading states in software exports are Karnataka, Maharashtra, Tamil Nadu, and Andhra Pradesh. Gujarat stands at a much lower position, with a little more than Rs. 1,000 crore of software exports in 2009-10.

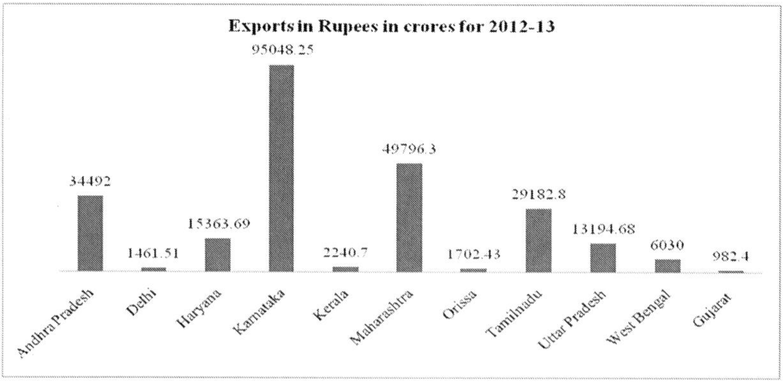

Source: STPI official website

Figure 8.12: Software Exports from STPI in Selected States

The Gujarat government has facilitated the development of IT parks by both the public and private sectors in the state. Interestingly, 13 out of 14 IT parks are located in the cities of Ahmedabad, Gandhinagar, and Vadodara. Furthermore, 12 of them have been promoted by real estate or infrastructure companies; and only two of them were built by genuine IT companies. One can argue that the IT parks in Gujarat are to promote the real estate sector rather than the IT sector. From Table 8.2, it is clear that the STP parks in Gujarat have not been able to fulfil the aims and objectives of the STPI act –increasing software production and revenue from ITeS services.

Table 8.2: State-wise software exports made by STPI registered units for last three years (in Cr)

State	2007-08	2008-09	2009-10
A P	26122.00	31039.00	27665.85
Gujarat	***681.00***	***1268.13***	***1035.00***
Haryana	10960.00	12410.00	14795.36
Karnataka	55000.00	70375.00	67100.00
Maharashtra	35374.00	42360.88	45709.34
Tamil Nadu	28295.00	28355.58	26363.51
U P	10695.21	10264.36	10590.43
W Bengal	4500.00	5129.00	5441.00

Source: NASSCOM

The Gujarat government has been trying very hard to attract investments in the IT sector from realty, finance, and banking sector companies through the highly propagated Vibrant Gujarat Summits every year. Many memoranda of understanding have been signed between stakeholders, but only a few of them have actually materialised. This means that the amount of FDI and local investments claimed by the government during the Vibrant Summits have remained largely on paper. Lately, many companies who have applied, identified land, or even made initial investments in the SEZs and IT parks are withdrawing because of the global slowdown.

What is on offer from Gujarat IT/ITeS?

The factors that make Gujarat a favourable place for the growth of the IT/ITeS sector in India are many. The entrepreneurial nature of Gujaratis and their high levels of professionalism have attracted many to invest in the IT sector. Gujarat has the best IT infrastructure in terms of internet bandwidth, network connectivity, surplus and uninterrupted 24/7 power supply etc. – all factors that are conducive to the growth of this sector. The lower cost of operations, particularly the cost of land, also makes it a destination of choice. The cities of Gujarat are relatively safe for female employees. Telephone and mobile density is comparatively high. The major cities of the state are well connected to both domestic and international centres by road, air and waterways. In addition to a vast army of English graduates, there is a pool of professionals which qualifications such as CA, CS, and MBAs etc. They can easily handle knowledge-based projects in finance, accounts, taxation, and international trade, which could help the growth of knowledge process outsourcing (KPOs) in Gujarat. The state government machinery is quite encouraging in providing a platform for the IT/ITeS sector to develop. There are strong and reliable links between Gujaratis living in Gujarat and NRGs (non-resident Gujaratis). This helps state-based IT/ITeS firms attract business from the US, the UK, and the EU on a regular basis.

Gujarat has the potential to become an IT hub because of five basic factors: business minded people; business friendly environment; easy market access; modern infrastructure and general competitiveness. The state has tremendous potential to grow in areas such as animation, gaming, cloud computing, e-health, visual effects, web design, IT maintenance and solutions, data mining, data processing and data management.

Gujarat's consumerist domestic market itself may boost the IT/ITeS sector. Online business could become a lucrative area for ITeS firms in Gujarat. E-governance programmes can generate a lot of demand for the sector within Gujarat and in surrounding states. Ever increasing mobile density, expanding e-commerce business, and a faster rate of urbanisation in Gujarat compared to other states are some of the unique factors that make this state a conducive place for the IT/ITeS sector to flourish.

The Government of Gujarat, in its IT policy of 2014, has promised a slew of incentives to the IT industry, including 100 per cent exemption from stamp duty and regulation fees, assistance in land purchase, total loan interest subsidy to MSME units and subsidy in the range of 5-7 per cent to others, 100 per cent exemption from electricity duty for five years, and many other initiatives to encourage companies to increase the industry turnover to USD 15 billion and to employ a million people in the next five years (IT Policy of Gujarat 2014-19). Last but not least, the Gujarat government has built the Gujarat International finance Tech-City (GIFT) on land measuring more than 500 acres between Ahmedabad and Gandhinagar cities. GIFT, conceptualised as a global financial and IT services hub, is the first of its kind in India and designed to be on par with or better than globally benchmarked financial centres. It aspires to catalyse India's large financial services potential by offering global and local financial services firms world-class infrastructure to attract talent from across the world (GIFT 2014).

Challenges ahead of India and Gujarat in the IT Sector

There are many challenges facing the IT sector in Gujarat. There is a shortage of technical and scientific manpower in the form of software and hardware engineers, IT assemblers, repairers, etc., in the state of Gujarat as compared to Karnataka, Tamilnadu, Andhra Pradesh, etc. Most of the well-known IT companies have already been successfully operating from Bangalore, Hyderabad, Noida, Pune, and Chennai for the last 10 years or more. Ahmedabad, Baroda, Surat and other cities of Gujarat remain only as second choices.

Wages in factories, such as textiles, chemicals, diamond cutting factories etc., in the cities of Gujarat are already higher than in many cities of other states. This discourages people from opting to work in the IT-BPO sector in Gujarat because relatively better reward alternatives are available in this western industrial state. Therefore, higher wages in Gujarat discourage IT/ITeS firms from setting up their bases here.

The Gujarat government, unlike those of Karnataka, Tamilnadu, Maharashtra, etc., has as of yet never had IT/ITeS industry in its list of priority areas. The state government has been encouraging the traditional manufacturing industries in which the state has been leading; therefore, the IT/ITeS sector has not received any substantial benefits, in the form of tax benefits or other concessions, like those it has received in the southern states.

Food and restaurants, health and education, banking and insurance, transport and communication, tourism, etc. are emerging areas in Gujarat wherein more and more employment opportunities are being created. Therefore, call centres are in constant search of workers to join them.

The Indian IT-BPO industry is still largely dependent on demand from the US, the UK and Continental Europe. More than 90 per cent of export demand comes from the western developed world. The economic slowdown in the US and some European countries has adversely affected

IT exports from India since 2009. Uncertainty in the rupee-dollar and rupee-euro exchange rates has also had a negative impact on the performance of the IT/ITeS sector in India. A fear regarding the future of the European Union due to the economic crisis has also caused some nervousness in the IT-BPO sector in India.

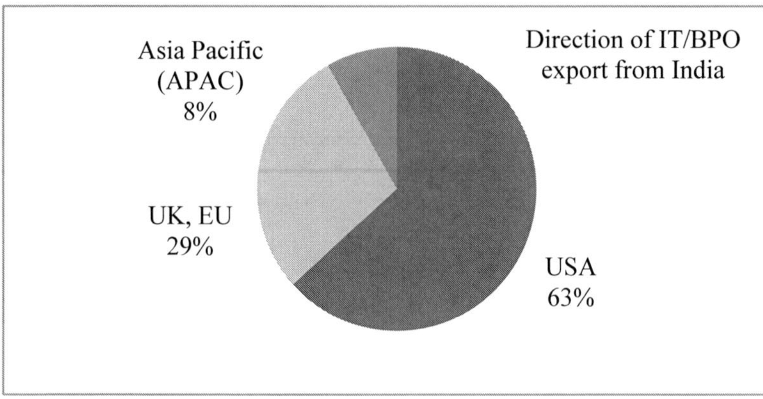

Source: Annual Report, 2011-12, Electronics and IT, MCIT, GOI

Figure 8.13: Direction of IT-BPO Export from India

Although there is huge potential for IT/ITeS within the country, the domestic market still remains largely untapped. Within India itself, there is plenty of scope for the IT business, in both the public and private sectors. E-commerce or online business, travel and hospitality within India could open the floodgates for the outsourcing industry in the country. Citizen-centric e-government services is another potential area that the industry could capitalise on to revive following the slowdown in demand from the West. The BPO sector in Gujarat could focus more on new areas such as e-education, e-health, online medical services etc. to push itself forward. With the Government of India planning to bridge the digital divide to connect 50,000 villages with broadband or Wi-Fi connectivity by the end of FY2014-15 and another 150,000 villages next year, there will be huge scope to fulfil the demand for ITeS from the rural areas of the country (TOI 2014). This would eventually take the call centres to smaller towns and tier II and III cities to serve the rural economy better in the long run.

There is a vast unexplored market for Indian IT/ITeS firms in Asia, Asia Pacific and Africa that could become a lifeline. Low end ITeS, like non-voice-based outsourcing business, can be profitably operated without any language barriers in such countries. The firms in this sector need to identify new markets in untapped regions of the globe. Indian IT firms need to identify the different types and natures of the IT/ITeS related requirements of different nations. If Indian IT/ITeS exports are well diversified in terms of export destination as well as composition, then the sector will be strengthened further and will be able to face newer challenges better than it does now.

References

Abraham, Vinoj. 2005. "Labour Productivity and Employment in the Indian Information and Communication Technology Industry." Unpublished PhD thesis, Jawaharlal Nehru University.

—. 2007. "Employee Attrition in Indian Software Industry: Patterns and Proximate Factors." *Labour and Development*. Vol. 12, No. 2 and Vol. 13, No. 1.

Abraham, Vinoj, and R.K. Sharma. 2005. "New Technology and the Emerging Labour Market: A Study of Indian IT Industry." *Indian Journal of Labour Economics.* Vol. 48, No. 4.

Basant, Rakesh. 1998. Review of *India's Software Industry: State Policy, Liberalisation and Industrial Development*, by Richard Heeks. *The Journal of Entrepreneurship*. Vol. 7, No. 1.

Basant, Rakesh, and Uma Rani. 2004. "Labour Market Deepening in the Indian Information Technology Industry: An Exploratory Analysis." *Working Paper Series*, Indian Institute of Management, Ahmedabad. WP 2004 06 06.

Desai, R.G. 2005. *Information Technology and Economic Growth.* Jaipur: Rawat Publications.

Gorden, Jim, and Poonam Gupta. 2003. "Understanding India's Services Revolution." Paper presented at the IMF-NCAER Conference on 'A Tale of Two Giants: India's and China's Experience with Reforms', New Delhi, November 14-16.

Ilavarasan, P. Vigneswara. 2008. "Software Work in India: A Labour Process." In *In an Outpost of the Global Economy: Work and Workers in India's Information Technology Industry,* edited by Carol Upadhya and A.R. Desai. New Delhi: Routledge.

Kumar, Nagesh, and K.J. Joseph. 2007. "*International Competitiveness and Knowledge Based Industries in India.*" New Delhi: Oxford University Press.

Lall, S. 2005. "Rethinking Industrial Strategy: The Role of the State in the Face of Globalization". In *Putting Development First,* edited by Kevin Gallagher. London: Zed Press.

McMillin, Divya C. 2006. "Outsourcing Indian Identity: Call Centres and Cultural Transformation in India." *Economic and Political Weekly.* Vol. 41, No. 3.

Noronha, Ernesto and Premilla D'cruz. 2006. "Organising Call Centre Agents: Emerging Issues". *Economic and Political Weekly.* Vol. 41, No. 21.

Pradhan, Jaya Prakash, and Vinoj Abraham. 2005. "Cultural and Social Impact of Outsourcing: Emerging Issues from India's Call Centres." *Harvard Asia Quarterly*. Vol. 9, No. 3.

Remesh, Babu P. 2004. "Cyber Coolies" in BPO: Insecurities and Vulnerabilities of Non-Standard Work" *Economic and Political Weekly*. Vol. 39, No. 5.

Rothboeck, S., M. Vijayabaskar, and V. Gayathri. 2001. "*Labour in the New Economy: The Case of the Indian Software Industry.*" International Labour Organisation, New Delhi.

Taganas, Rey A. L. and Vijay Kumar Kaul. 2006. "Innovation Systems in India's IT Industry: An Empirical Investigation". *Economic and Political Weekly*. Vol. 41, No. 39.

Upadhyay, Carol. 2007. "Employment, Exclusion and "Merit" in the Indian IT Industry." *Economic and Political Weekly*. Vol. 42, No. 20.

Websites

GESIA. 2014. "About us." Accessed December 16, 2014. http://www.gesia.org/aboutus.php.

GIFT. 2014. Accessed on December 16, 2014. http://giftgujarat.in/faq.aspx.

NASSCOM. 2012. "NASSCOM-Everest India, 'BPO Study Roadmap 2012." Accessed December 16, 2014. http://www.nasscom.in/sites/default/files/upload/55783/NASSCOM_Everest_India_BPO_Study_Exec_Summary.pdf.

Mishra, *Law Kumar. 2014.* "Broadband connection to 50,000 villages this financial year: Ravi Shankar Prasad." TNN Nov 8. Accessed December 16, 2014. http://timesofindia.indiatimes.com/city/patna/Broadband-connection-to-50000-villages-this-FY-Min/articleshow/45083644.cms.

"Gujarat announces slew of industry incentives in new IT policy." *ZeeNews*, November 15, 2014. Accessed December 16, 2014 http://zeenews.india.com/news/gujarat/gujarat-announces-slew-of-industry-incentives-in-new-it-policy_1499776.html.

"Gujarat declares new IT/ITES policy; targets 15-fold turnover jump by 2020." *The Indian Express*, November 15. Accessed December 16, 2014. http://indianexpress.com/article/business/economy/gujarat-declares-new-itites-policy-targets-15-fold-turnover-jump-by-2020/.

Reports

MICT. 2011-12. "Annual Report 2011-12, Electronics and Information Technology, Ministry of Information and Communication Technology." Accessed December 16, 2014. http://deity.gov.in/sites/upload_files/dit/files/downloads/annualreports/AnnualReport_2011-12/AnnualReportE_2011-12_8412.pdf.

NASSCOM. 2014. "NASSCOM Annual Report 2013-2014." Accessed on December 16, 2014. http://www.nasscom.in/sites/default/files/NASSCOM%20Annual%20Report%202013-14.pdf.

STPI. 1991. STPI Annual Reports. Accessed on December 16, 2014. http://www.stpi.in/index1.php?langid=1&level=0&linkid=134&lid=192.

THOLONS. 2013. "Tholons 2014 Tholons Top 100 Outsourcing Destinations: Ranking." Accessed December 16, 2014. http://www.tholons.com/nl_pdf/Whitepaper_December_2013.pdf.

UNCTAD. 2012. "Information Economy Report 2012: The Software Industry and Developing Countries." Accessed December 16, 2014. http://unctad.org/en/pages/PublicationWebflyer.aspx?publicationid=271.

"IT/ITeS Policy of Maharashtra 2009." Government of Maharashtra. Accessed on December 16, 2014. https://www.maharashtra.gov.in/PDF/itpolicy.pdf.

"IT/ITeS Policy of Maharashtra 2003". Government of Maharashtra. Accessed on December 16, 2014. http://www.bcasonline.org/referencer%20file/itesPolicy2003.pdf.

"IT and ITES Policy 2007." Department of Information Technology and Communication, Government of Rajasthan. Accessed December 16, 2014. http://vikaspedia.in/e-governance/national-e-governance-plan/it-policy_rajasthan.

Appendix 8.1

The following is a list of IT Parks in Gujarat: (Source: STPI official website)

1) M/s Aqualine Properties Pvt. Ltd. (Raheja Group), Koba, Gandhinagar
2) M/s Ganesh Infrastructure Pvt. Ltd., Dascroi, Ahmedabad
3) M/s City Gold Realties Pvt. Ltd., Sanand Ahmedabad
4) M/s Shivganga Real Estate Holders Pvt. Ltd., Ahmedabad
5) M/s Calica Construction & Impex Pvt. Ltd., Ognej. Ahmedabad
6) M/s Adani Township & Real Estate Company Pvt. Ltd., Dantali, Ahmedabad
7) M/s Nipiam Infotech Pvt. Ltd., Vaghodia, Vadodara
8) M/s Gujarat Industrial Development Corporation, Near Infocity, Gandhinagar
9) Tata Consultancy Services Ltd., Near Infocity, Gandhinagar
10) M/s SGV Infrastructure Pvt. Ltd., Ahmedabad
11) M/s Larsen & Toubro Limited., Vadodara
12) M/s Strength Real Estate Pvt. Ltd., Vadodara
13) Myron Realtors Private Ltd., Ahmedabad
14) Mexus Corporation Pvt. Ltd., Valsad

CHAPTER NINE

AN ANALYSIS OF THE INSURANCE SECTOR: PENETRATION PERSPECTIVE IN INDIA

PRIYANKA GUPTA AND VANI AGGARWAL[1]

Overview of the Insurance Sector

Insurance is defined as the equitable transfer of the risk of loss from one entity to another, in exchange for a payment, called a *premium* (NCAER). Insurance is a form of risk management, which is used to hedge or cover the risk of a contingent and uncertain loss. The insurance sector acts as a mobilizer of savings, a financial intermediary, a promoter of investment activities, a stabilizer of financial markets and a risk manager in the economy. At present, the insurance sector[2] in India has a share of 17.1 per cent in total gross domestic product (GDP), and recorded a healthy growth rate of 16.82 per cent in 2012-13. According to IBEF, India ranked 10th among 156 countries in the life insurance business, with a share of 2.3 per cent during 2011-12, and 19th among 156 countries in the non-life premium business, with a share of 0.62 per cent in 2011-12 (IBEF 2013).

According to the Financial Stability Forum,[3] insurance services are categorized into three major groups: life insurance, non-life insurance and

---

[1] The authors are grateful to Dr. Murali Kallummal, Associate Professor, Centre for WTO Studies, and Dr. Pralok Gupta, Assistant Professor, Centre for WTO Studies, IIFT, New Delhi, for their valuable suggestions.

[2] Insurance includes finance, insurance, real estate and business services.

[3] The Financial Stability Forum (FSF) brings together senior representatives of national financial authorities, international financial institutions, international regulatory and supervisory groupings (including sector specific ones), committees of central bank experts and the European Central Bank. It was convened in April 1999 to promote international financial stability through information exchange and international co-operation in financial supervision and surveillance. The FSF seeks to coordinate the efforts of these various bodies to promote international financial

reinsurance. The life insurance sector helps in providing risk cover, investment and tax planning for individuals; the non-life insurance industry provides a risk cover for assets, and reinsurance acts as "insurance for insurers" or "stop-loss insurance”. The development of the life insurance market is playing an increasingly substantial role within the insurance industry due to the existence of an insurance-growth relationship, with the increased share of the insurance sector in the financial sector (Beck and Webb 2003).

The services sector has the largest share in India’s GDP (Economic Survey 2012-13). The insurance sector contributes 17 per cent to the services sector, which has high growth potential (Appendix 9.1). There is significant untapped potential in various segments of the insurance market, as the Indian insurance industry is highly protected and large segments of the economy are underinsured in terms of per capita insurance premiums and because of low penetration. While the nation is highly exposed to natural catastrophes, insurance cover to mitigate the negative financial consequences of these adverse events is still inadequate. Foreign and private players can bridge the gap between the actual and potential insurance markets.

In the life insurance business, the sector is monopolized by the Life Insurance Corporation of India (LIC), which has captured 71 per cent of the market in total premiums and 72 per cent of the market in first year premiums, as opposed to only 29 per cent and 28 per cent of the market in total premiums and first year premiums respectively served by private players. In the non-life insurance business, the public sector also dominates the market, with a share of 58 per cent, while the private sector caters to 43 per cent of the market (Appendix 9.2).

The rising importance of insurance in the globalized world is evident from the increased number of players in both the domestic and international markets (IRDA 2011). India, being one of the fastest-growing economies in the world, after China, and an up-and-coming, attractive foreign direct investment (FDI) destination for major developed economies, has the potential to significantly increase the size of its insurance industry. In 2012-13, the services sector (financial and non-financial) constituted around 25 per cent of FDI equity inflows, compared to 14.3 per cent in 2011-12 (DIPP 2012). Increasing disposable income, coupled with the high potential demand for insurance offerings, has opened many doors for both domestic and foreign insurers. Telecommunications, computer software and

---

stability, improve the functioning of markets, and reduce systemic risk. See http://www.fsforum.org.

hardware, housing and real estate and construction are the major sectors that attract various modes of capital inflows from foreign investors (Appendix 9.3).

FDI could help increase insurance penetration in the economy by developing the life and non-life insurance markets and accessing more insurance offices with large per capita numbers of agents in India (Sinha et al 2012). Further, foreign players have high levels of expertise and technical know-how in the reinsurance business. In India, General Insurance Corporation (GIC) is the sole reinsurer, which implies immense opportunity for other private and foreign players to tap the reinsurance market. FDI also brings in huge capital, which can be a source of foreign exchange reserves. Stable foreign exchange inflows in the form of FDI could bridge the infrastructure deficit and untapped potential in the Indian insurance market.

Evolution of the Insurance Sector: A Retrospect

Before deregulation in 1999, the Indian insurance industry was dominated by state-owned insurers, namely LIC for life insurance, and GIC with its four subsidiaries for general insurance. The rising importance of insurance in the Indian market paved the way for private and foreign players (subject to a cap of 26 per cent) following the recommendations of the R.N. Malhotra committee report (1994), which supported the liberalization of the insurance sector. Table 9.1 provides the important developments in the evolution of the Indian insurance industry.

Table 9.1: Important Developments in the History of the Indian Insurance Industry[4]

1912	The Life Insurance Companies Act was passed, making it mandatory for companies to get their premium rate tables certified by an actuary.
1938	The Insurance Act of 1938 became the first legislation governing all forms of insurance to provide strict state control over the insurance business.
1956	Life insurance in India was completely nationalized on January 19th by means of the Life Insurance Corporation Act. All 245 existing companies operating in the country were merged into one entity, namely the Life Insurance Corporation of India (LIC).

[4] NCAER survey report on Insurance Awareness Campaign.

1957	The General Insurance Council, a wing of the Insurance Association of India, was formed and framed a code of conduct for ensuring fair conduct and sound business practices.
1968	The Insurance Act of 1938 was amended to regulate investments and set minimum solvency margins. The Tariff Advisory Committee was also set up.
1972	The General Insurance Business (Nationalization) Act was passed. With effect from January 1st, 1973, 107 companies were amalgamated and grouped into four companies, namely National Insurance Company Ltd., Oriental Insurance Company Ltd., New India Assurance Company Ltd and United India Insurance Company Ltd.
1993	The Government of India set up a committee under the chairmanship of Sh. R.N. Malhotra, the then Governor of the Reserve Bank of India, to propose recommendations for reforms in the insurance sector that would complement the reforms in the financial sector.
1994	The committee recommended that entry of the private sector into the insurance sector be permitted and that foreign companies be allowed entry by floating Indian companies, preferably as joint ventures with Indian partners.
1996	Following the recommendations of the Malhotra Committee, an interim Insurance Regulatory Authority was set up.
1999	The Insurance Regulatory and Development Authority (IRDA) was created as an autonomous body to regulate and develop the insurance industry. The IRDA was incorporated as a statutory body in April 2000. The key objective of IRDA is to promote competition in order to improve customer satisfaction through increased customer choice and lower premiums, while ensuring the financial security of the insurance market. The IRDA deregulated the insurance sector and permitted the entry of private companies. Foreign investment was also allowed and capped at 26 per cent holding in Indian insurance companies.
2006	The Actuaries Act was passed to give the profession statutory status on par with chartered accountants, notaries, cost and works accountants, advocates, architects and company secretaries.

Source: Authors' compilation

With the introduction of the Insurance Regulatory and Development Authority Act in 1999, India abandoned public sector exclusivity in the insurance industry in favour of market-driven competition. This was a major step and led to the entry of international insurers, leading to a proliferation of innovative products and distribution channels. The entry of multinationals also helped lift supervisory standards in the industry to a higher level. The insurance sector was further liberalized recently, with the limit on FDI through the automatic route raised to 26 per cent with effect from April 2013 (DIPP 2014).[5]

India's GATS Commitments on Insurance Services

The globalization of trade in services is an important objective for India as a signatory to the agreement establishing the World Trade Organization. The WTO W/120 sectoral classification list[6] breaks down financial services into (a) all insurance and insurance related services and (b) banking and other financial services. The former is further broken down into: life, accident and health insurance services; non-life insurance services; reinsurance and retrocession; insurance intermediation, and services auxiliary to insurance.

Under GATS, there are four modes of supply: 1) Mode 1 – cross-border supply;[7] 2) Mode 2 – Consumption abroad;[8] 3) Mode 3 – commercial presence[9] and 4) Mode 4 – presence of natural persons,[10]

---

[5] http://dipp.nic.in/English/Policies/FDI_Circular_2014.pdf.

[6] Note that the W/120 differs from the CPC in the following ways (among others): (a) accident and health insurance are included in "life" insurance instead of "non-life" insurance, as in the CPC; (b) reinsurance and retrocession, which were not specifically mentioned in the CPC and were part of a residual category "other insurance services n.e.c.", have been separated out; (c) pension fund management services are set apart from life insurance services and included in asset management services under "banking and other financial services" and (d) "insurance brokering and agency services" and other services auxiliary to insurance have been regrouped together as a subsector of insurance services. As regards the GATS Annex on Financial Services, it goes a step further in the disaggregation of "services auxiliary to insurance" in W/120 by separating "intermediation such as brokerage and agency" from auxiliary services and by specifying explicitly some of those auxiliary services, namely consultancy, actuarial, risk assessment and claim settlement services.

[7] From the territory of one member country into the territory of any other member country.

[8] In the territory of one member country to the service consumer of any other member country.

[9] By a service supplier of one member country, through commercial presence, in the territory of any other member country.

which facilitate trade in services. India's GATS commitments on the four modes of supply of insurance services are provided in Table 9.2.

Table 9.2: India's GATS commitments on insurance and insurance-related services

Sub-sector	Limitations on Market Access	Limitations on National Treatment
Non-life, limited to insurance of freight Ex. 5(a)(i)(B)	1) Unbound except in the case of insurance of freight, where there is no requirement that goods in transit to and from India should be insured with Indian insurance companies only. Insurance is taken out by the buyer or seller in accordance with the terms of the contract. This position will be maintained. Once under a contract, the Indian importer or exporter agrees to assume responsibility for insurance, such as in the case of f.o.b. contracts for imports into India or c.i.f. contracts for exports from India. Insurance has to be taken out with an Indian insurance company.	1) Unbound.
	2) Unbound	2) Unbound.
	3) Unbound	3) Unbound.
	4) Unbound except as indicated in the horizontal section.	4) Unbound except as indicated in the horizontal section.
Reinsurance and retrocession 5 (a)(ii)	1) Reinsurance can be taken with foreign reinsurers to the extent of the residual uncovered risk after obligatory or statutory placements domestically with Indian insurance companies.	1) Unbound.
	2) Reinsurance can be taken with foreign reinsurers to the extent of the residual uncovered risk after obligatory or statutory placements domestically with Indian insurance companies.	2) Unbound.

[10] By a service supplier of one member country, through the presence of natural persons in the territory of any other member country.

	3) Unbound.	3) Unbound.
	4) Unbound except as indicated in the horizontal section.	4) Unbound except as indicated in the horizontal section.
Insurance intermediation, limited to reinsurance Ex. 5(a)(iii)	1) Reinsurance of domestic risks can be placed with foreign reinsurers through overseas brokers, to the extent mentioned under reinsurance and retrocession.	1) Unbound.
	2) Reinsurance of domestic risks can be placed with foreign reinsurers through overseas brokers, to the extent mentioned under reinsurance and retrocession.	2) Unbound.
	3) (i) Overseas brokers are allowed to have resident representatives and representative offices who can procure reinsurance business from Indian insurance companies to the extent mentioned above. They can also place reinsurance business from abroad with Indian insurance companies. (ii) Except for the business indicated above, the resident representatives and representative offices cannot undertake any other activity in India. (iii) All expenses of the resident representatives and representative offices have to be met by remittances from abroad and no income can be received in India from Indian residents.	3) Unbound.
	4) Unbound except as indicated in the horizontal section.	4) Unbound except as indicated in the horizontal section.

Source: WTO

Literature Review

The insurance sector is a central element of the development matrix and is considered one of the key pillars of financial services. There is growing empirical literature and research seeking to assess the relationship between the macroeconomic performance of the insurance sector and economic growth. A well-functioning insurance sector plays a crucial role in economic development, not just at a macroeconomic level, but also in terms of the activities of individuals and businesses (UNCTAD 2007). A sound national insurance sector represents an essential feature of a proper economic system, contributing to economic growth and fostering high employment (UNCTAD 1964). Within a given country, the development of an insurance market can be examined in terms of the level of insurance penetration. A higher insurance penetration level would indicate a more developed insurance market within the economy (Lloyd's Report 2012).

Many researchers and academicians have tried to exploit the relationship between per capita GDP and insurance penetration at different stages of development and growth in per capita GDP. Carter, Dickinson (1992) and Enz (2000) point out that "insurance penetration cannot go on increasing at the same pace forever with per capita income". Enz (2000) provided a non-linear S-curve relationship between insurance penetration and per capita GDP. The study also analyzed insurance penetration (life and non-life insurance) with per capita income by plotting a graph for selected countries which showed that there exists a level of per capita income at which the penetration reaches its maxima. Beyond the point of maxima, insurance penetration increases at a decreasing rate with the increase in the level of per capita GDP.

Packard (2008) studied the ordinary growth model, which postulated that the increase in insurance penetration is accompanied by different levels of GDP per capita. For instance, low GDP per capita correlates with a slow rate of increase of insurance penetration; increasing GDP per capita leads to a high rate of increase of insurance penetration; however, at the highest levels of GDP per capita, the rate of insurance penetration slows and levels off. The above studies support the argument that there is an important relationship between insurance penetration and the per capita GDP of a country; however, it does not preclude the presence of other factors (both demand- and supply-driven) that are likely to influence the level of penetration in different countries/states. IRDA (2011) highlights demand-driven factors such as the socio-demographic characteristics and the risk appetite of policy holders, which influence insurance penetration and vary across states and union territories (UTs) in India, while Sinha et al (2012) mention supply-driven factors such as per capita number of agents and per capita number of insurance offices, which affect insurance penetration in an economy.

Recent Trends and Analysis of the Insurance Sector

The performance of the insurance sector can be assessed with reference to two parameters: insurance penetration and insurance density. This study focuses on the trends in insurance penetration and insurance density in India with an analysis of the factors responsible for changing trends over the time period 1990-2011.

Insurance Penetration

Insurance penetration explains the growth of premiums with the growth of the gross domestic product in the economy. It is measured as a ratio of premium to GDP (IRDA 2011-12). Insurance penetration (both life and non-life) in the post-liberalization period is shown in Figure 9.1. Total insurance penetration has increased from 1.90 per cent in 1990 to 4.10 per cent in 2011, although penetration remained stagnant for the period of 1990 (1.90 per cent) to 1999 (1.93 per cent). Life insurance dominates insurance penetration in India; however, its share has been declining since 2010. It increased from 1.41 per cent in 1990 to 4.40 per cent in 2010 and then declined to 3.40 per cent in 2011, while the share of non-life insurance penetration in total insurance penetration hovered around 1 per cent; it increased from 0.5 per cent in 1990 to 0.7 per cent in 2011.

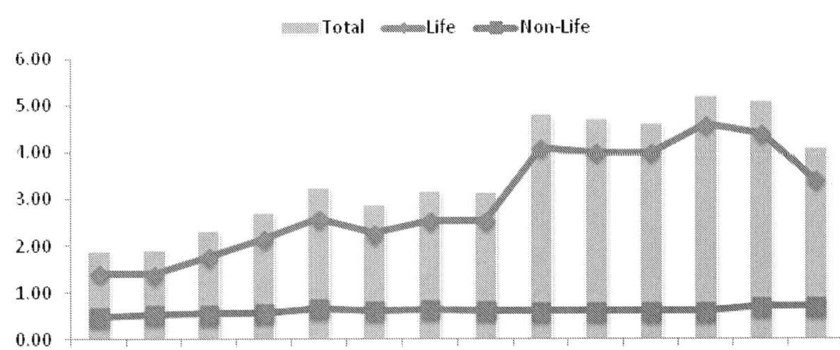

Source: Swiss Re, Various Issues[11]

Figure 9.1: Insurance penetration in India (in per cent)[12]

[11] IRDA, Annual Report 2011-12.

[12] Appendix 9.4.

The opening up of the insurance sector since 2000 has marked a consistent increase in total penetration levels. India's growing consumer class, rising insurance awareness, and increasing domestic savings and investments are among the most critical factors that have positively driven the market penetration of insurance products among various consumer segments. However, there are many impediments, such as lack of awareness and financial illiteracy, which hamper the growth of the insurance industry. The industry penetration level is on the downward path since 2010 having declined from 5.10 per cent in 2010 to 4.10 per cent in 2011. Imparting financial literacy, incentivizing Indian households to transfer savings from physical assets to financial assets and taking the distribution network to rural areas will help bring more and more individuals within the insurance ambit.

Figure 9.2 indicates that there has been a declining trend in the financial savings of households as percentage of total gross domestic savings (GDS). Both domestic and international factors have contributed to the sluggish growth of financial savings. The consistent and persistent double digit inflation in the Indian economy is largely responsible for the biased nature of savings in physical assets, as it acts as a hedge against inflation.

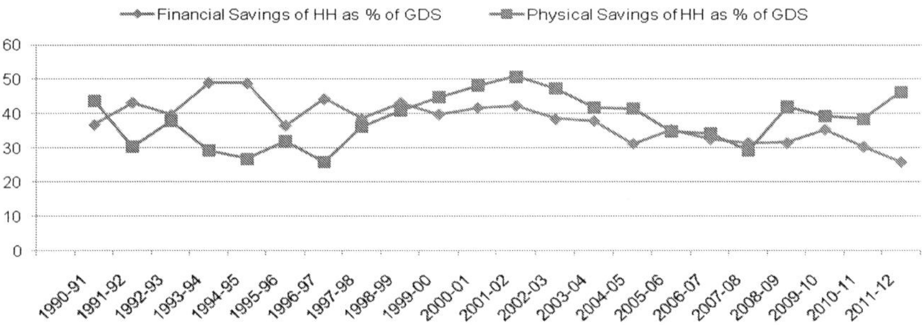

Source: RBI

Figure 9.2: Financial and physical savings as % of GDS

Physical and financial savings as a percentage of GDS have shown divergent trends over the studied period of time. While physical savings have shown an upward trend during the post-crisis period (2009-10), financial savings have shown a declining trend.

Empirical evidence and investigation show that there is a relationship between per capita GDP and total insurance penetration. Data also indicate that there is a positive relationship (Figure 9.3); penetration increased from 1.90 per cent in 1990 to 5.10 per cent in 2010; similarly, per capita GDP rose from Rs. 6,987.03 in 1990 to Rs. 65,727.77 in 2010. In 2011, growth in insurance penetration declined while per capita GDP followed the same upward trend. However, there are various demand (socio-demographic characteristics of policy holders, risk appetites, etc.) and supply (quality of distribution channels, product innovation, etc.) driven factors that could boost insurance penetration levels in India (IRDA). With the help of these factors, it is likely that insurance penetration in the country will increase.

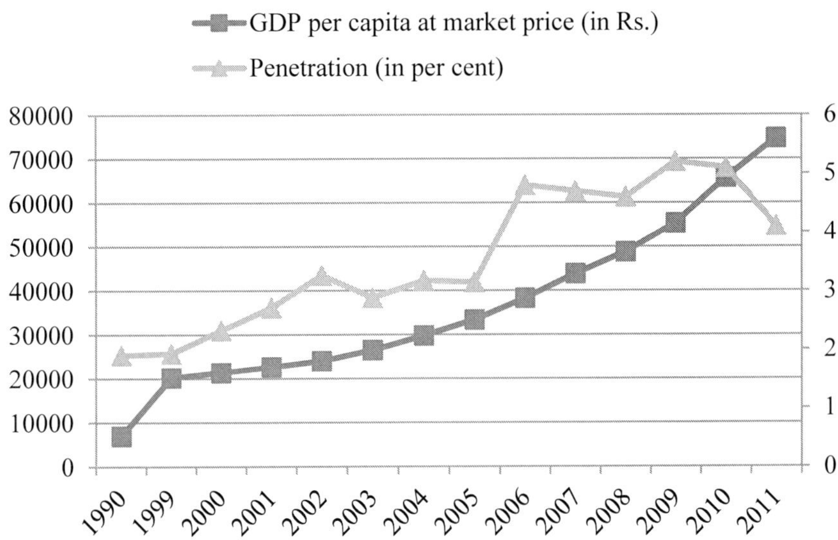

Source: IRDA and RBI

Figure 9.3: Per Capita GDP and Insurance Penetration in India[13]

State-Group Wise Insurance Penetration of Individual New Businesses

To study the pattern of insurance penetration in states according to the per capita NSDP, Indian states have been classified into three broad income groups, namely low-income, middle-income and high-income states, using the average per capita NSDP from 2006-07 to 2011-12 (Appendix 9.6). This study examines the relationship between the per

[13] Appendix 9.5.

capita NSDP of low-income states, middle-income states and high-income states and insurance penetration (new business) over the years.

Figure 9.4 shows the relationship between insurance penetration of new businesses and per capita NSDP of low-, middle- and high-income states. It shows that from 2006-07 to 2011-12, the penetration levels in the low-income states of India declined with respect to per capita NSDP, implying that as the average income of low-income states rises, the penetration of new businesses declined. Similarly, in the high-income states (Haryana, Puducherry, Sikkim, Chandigarh, Delhi, Goa), the level of penetration shows a downward slope as states move on to a higher income. Middle-income states also follow a similar pattern, i.e. a higher growth of income implies lower insurance penetration. Thus, the data shows a negative relationship between insurance penetration of new businesses and per capita state GDP. It has been observed that Indian states are biased towards physical savings rather than financial savings, which has contributed to a lower level of new business insurance penetration in these states. "*Insurance is largely used as a tax saving tool, rather than for protection against risk. There is need to reorient the consumer about the benefits of life insurance for both financial protection as well as for long-term wealth creation*" (NCAER 2011). There is a potential need to concentrate on the issue of financial awareness, as well as to inculcate the habit of being insured to hedge against risks and uncertainties.

An international comparison of penetration levels suggest that insurance penetration in India, which stands at 4.1 per cent, was well below the world average of 6.6 per cent in 2011. It is interesting to note that insurance penetration in India is way below penetration levels in major Asian economies, such as Hong-Kong, Japan, Taiwan, South Korea, Malaysia and Singapore, although it is above China, Pakistan and Sri Lanka (Table 9.3).

Table 9.3: International Comparison of Insurance Penetration (in per cent)

Countries	2010			2011		
	Total	**Life**	**Non-Life**	**Total**	**Life**	**Non-Life**
Australia	5.9	3.1	2.8	6.0	3.0	3.0
Brazil	3.1	1.6	1.5	3.2	1.7	1.5
France	10.5	7.4	3.1	9.5	6.2	3.3
Germany	7.2	3.5	3.7	6.8	3.2	3.6
Russia	2.3	0.0	2.3	2.4	0.1	2.3
South Africa	14.8	12.0	2.8	12.9	10.2	2.7
Switzerland	9.9	5.5	4.4	10.0	5.5	4.5
United Kingdom	12.4	9.5	2.9	11.8	8.7	3.1
United States	8.0	3.5	4.5	8.1	3.6	4.5
Asian Countries						
Bangladesh	0.9	0.7	0.2	0.9	0.7	0.2
Hong Kong	11.4	10.1	1.4	11.4	10.1	1.4
India	**5.1**	**4.4**	**0.7**	**4.1**	**3.4**	**0.7**
Japan	10.1	8.0	2.1	11.0	8.8	2.2
Malaysia	4.8	3.2	1.6	5.1	3.3	1.8
Pakistan	0.7	0.3	0.3	0.7	0.4	0.3
PR China	3.8	2.5	1.3	3.0	1.8	1.2
Singapore	6.1	4.6	1.6	5.9	4.3	1.5
South Korea	11.2	7.0	4.2	11.6	7.0	4.6
Sri Lanka	1.4	0.6	0.9	1.2	0.6	0.6
Taiwan	18.4	15.4	3.0	17.0	13.9	3.1
Thailand	4.3	2.6	1.7	4.4	2.7	1.7
World	**6.9**	**4.0**	**2.9**	**6.6**	**3.8**	**2.8**

Source: Swiss Re, Sigma Volumes 2/2011 and 3/2012

Low Income States of India, 2006-11

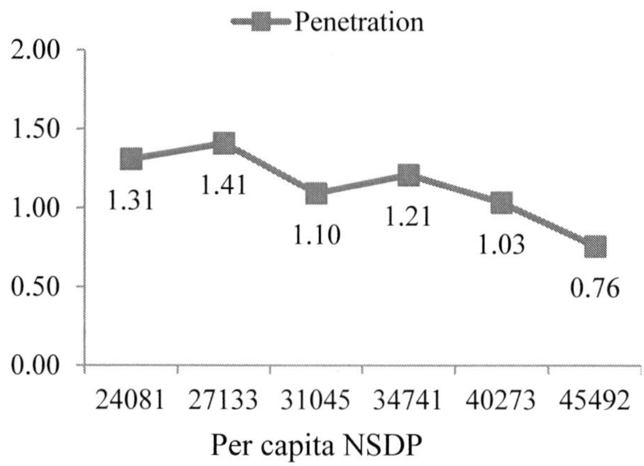

Middle Income States of India, 2006-11

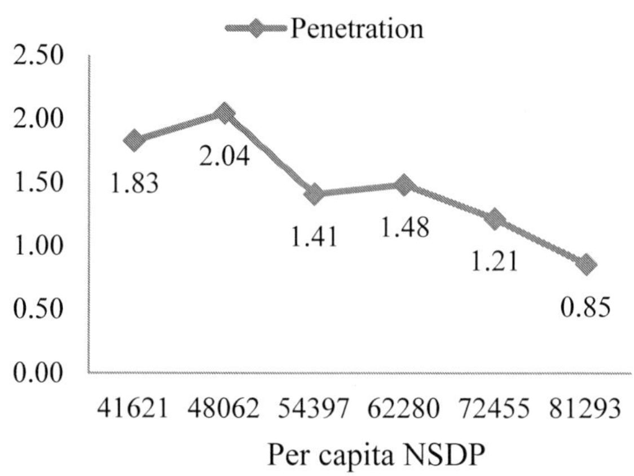

High Income States of India, 2006-11

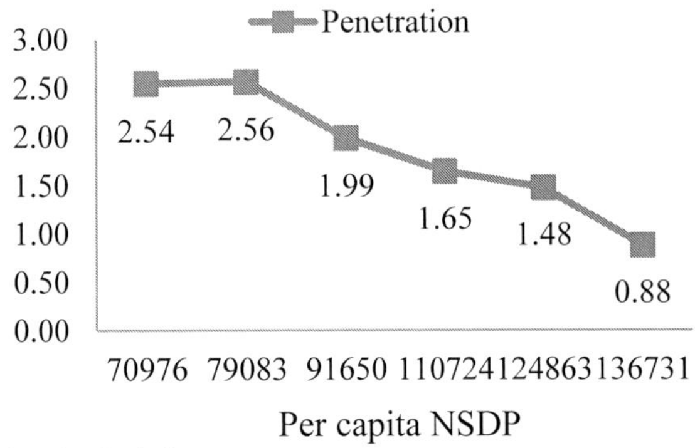

Source: Authors' calculation

Figure 9.4: Insurance penetration of new businesses and per capita NSDP of low-, middle- and high-income states[14]

Insurance Density

Insurance density is known as per capita premium and measured as the ratio of premium (in USD) to total population (IRDA 2011-12). Since liberalization, total insurance density has shown an upward trend; it increased from USD 11.50 in 2001 to USD 59 in 2011. Similarly, life insurance density shows a surge from 2001 (USD 9.10) to 2010 (USD 55.70), although in 2011, it fell to USD 49 (Figure 9.5). The life insurance sector captures the greater share of total insurance density.

Non-life insurance density shows an upward trend after the privatization of the insurance sector. With the entry of private players, non-life insurance density in India rose from USD 2.40 in 2001 to USD 10 in 2011.

Table 9.4 shows an international comparison of insurance density in 2011. This international comparison suggests that the density in India, which stands at USD 59, is well below the world average of USD 661 in 2011. It is interesting to note that insurance density in China is approximately three times as high as in India due to steady economic growth. However, both countries are markedly below the world average of USD 628. Pakistan, Sri Lanka and Bangladesh are laggards in terms of their insurance density.

---

[14] Appendix 9.7.

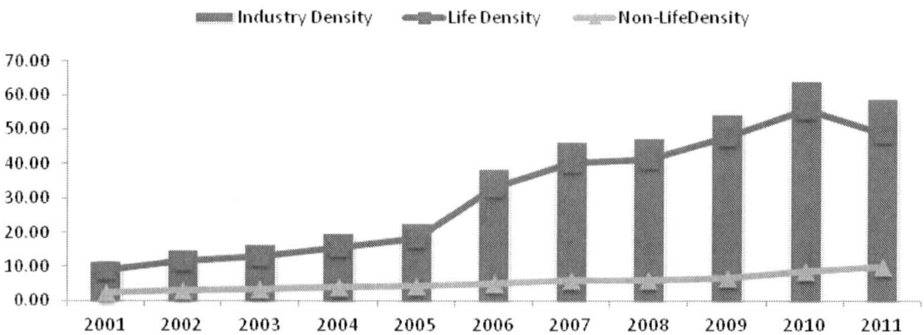

Source: Swiss Re, Various Issues[15]

Figure 9.5: Insurance Density in India (in USD)[16]

Table 9.4: International Comparison of Insurance Density (in USD)

Countries	2010			2011		
	Total	Life	Non-Life	Total	Life	Non-Life
Australia	3369.2	1766.3	1603.0	4094.0	2077.0	2017.0
Brazil	327.6	169.9	157.7	398.0	208.0	189.0
France	4186.6	2937.6	1249.0	4041.0	2638.0	1403.0
Germany	2903.8	1402.2	1501.6	2967.0	1389.0	1578.0
Russia	296.8	6.4	290.4	303.0	8.0	295.0
South Africa	1054.7	854.6	200.1	1037.0	823.0	215.0
Switzerland	6633.7	3666.8	2966.9	8012.0	4421.0	3591.0
United Kingdom	4496.6	3436.3	1060.2	4535.0	3347.0	1188.0
United States	3758.9	1631.8	2127.2	3846.0	1716.0	2130.0
Asian Countries						
Bangladesh	5.8	4.4	1.4	7.0	5.0	2.0
Hong Kong	3635.5	3197.3	438.2	3904.0	3442.0	462.0
India	**64.4**	**55.7**	**8.7**	**59.0**	**49.0**	**10.0**
Japan	4390.2	3472.8	917.4	5169.0	4138.0	1031.0
Malaysia	421.1	282.8	138.3	502.0	328.0	175.0
Pakistan	6.1	3.2	2.9	8.0	4.0	4.0

[15] IRDA, Annual Report 2011-12.
[16] Appendix 9.4.

PR China	158.4	105.5	52.9	163.0	99.0	64.0
Singapore	2823.4	2101.4	722.1	3106.0	2296.0	810.0
South Korea	2339.4	1454.3	885.1	2661.0	1615.0	1045.0
Sri Lanka	34.2	13.7	20.6	33.0	15.0	18.0
Taiwan	3296.2	2756.8	539.3	3371.0	2757.0	614.0
Thailand	199.4	121.9	77.5	222.0	134.0	88.0
World	**627.3**	**364.3**	**263.0**	**661.0**	**378.0**	**283.0**

Source: Swiss Re, Sigma Volumes 2/2011 and 3/2012

Conclusion

The insurance sector has immense potential in terms of contribution to growth momentum. Underinsured and unsaturated markets need to be tapped in order to realize its full impact on the Indian economy. This study identifies the low level of insurance penetration and density levels in India vis-à-vis various advanced and emerging economies. It has also shown the correlation between insurance penetration and economic development. India comprises 28 states and seven UTs, with varied NSDPs and levels of penetration and density. The variation observed across states and UTs can be attributed to various demand- and supply-driven factors. The increased penetration with the opening up of the sector in 2000 gives a clear indication that private and foreign players have the ability to enhance the size of the insurance market and participation in it.

The insurance sector demands huge investment, working capital[17] and in-depth knowledge of the market. The maturity period for generating profits in the insurance industry, both life and non-life, is quite long, which means the efficiency of the insurance market is underestimated.

Low and uneven development of insurance, especially in the non-life line of business, increases the level of risk in economic decisions taken by individuals and firms, which hampers economic activities. The declining level of penetration of new business in all state categories is a matter for concern. The regulatory environment for insurance should encourage risk-based pricing. The government should act as a promoter and facilitator of insurance services by privatizing and liberalizing the insurance sector so that levels of insurance in the country can improve in relation to the standards in the international market.

[17] Working capital refers to current assets net of liabilities.

References

Andrade, Nigel, Balasubramanian, Ramnath, Ehrbeck, Tilman, and Anu Madgavkar. 2012. "India Life Insurance 2012: Fortune Favors the Bold." McKinsey & Company Report.

Annual Report of Insurance Regulatory and Development Authority. Government of India. Various Issues.

Arkell, Julian. 2011. "The essential role of Insurance services for Trade and Development." A Primer from the Geneva Association's Programme on Regulation and Supervision.

Banga, Rashmi. 2005. "Foreign Direct Investment in Services: Implications for Developing Countries." *Asia-Pacific Trade and Investment Review* Vol. 1, No. 2.

Bhat, Ramesh. 2005. "Insurance Industry in India: Structure, Performance, and Future Challenges." *Vikalpa* Vol. 30, No 3.

Carter, R. L., and Dickinson. 1992. *Obstacles to the Liberalization of Trade in Insurance*. London: Harvester Wheatsheaf.

De, Prabir, and Ajitava Raychaudhuri. 2008. "Is India's services trade pro-poor? A Simultaneous Approach." *Macao Regional Knowledge Hub Working Papers*, No. 16.

Enz, R. 2000. "The S-Curve Relation between Per-Capita Income and Insurance Penetration." *Geneva Papers on Risk and Insurance* Vol. 25, No.3, 396-406.

Estimates of Annual National Income. Press Information Bureau Government of India. Various Issues.

India Brand Equity Foundation Reports. Various Issues

Indian Insurance Sector: Innovate Now or Stagnate, 2011. Deloitte Report.

Lloyd's Global Underinsurance Report, 2012.

Mukherjee, Arpita. 2012. "Services Sector in India: Trends, Issues and Way Forward." Draft paper, *Indian Council for Research on International Economic Relations*.

Prasad and Sathish. 2010. *Policy for India's Services Sector*. Department of Economic Affairs, Ministry of Finance, Government of India.

Pre-launch Report of Insurance Campaign Survey Awareness. 2011. National Council of Applied Economic Research and Insurance Regulatory Development Authority.

Roy, Sumit. 2011. *Statistics on Trade in Services in India*, Reserve Bank of India.

Sen Gupta, Abhijit. 2007. "Banking and Insurance Services Liberalization in the Context of an Indo-EU Trade and Investment Agreement." *Indian Council for Research on International Economic Relations.*

Sinha, R. K., Nizamuddin M. M., and Alam, I. 2012. *An Investigation of insurance penetration and density of India by geography.* 16th Annual Conference of Asia-Pacific Risk and Insurance Association (APRIA), Seoul, South Korea.

Swiss Re: Various Sigma Reports.

Trade and Development aspects of Insurance Services and Regulatory Frameworks. 2007. United Nations Conference on Trade and Development.

Appendix 9.1

Share and Growth of India's Services Sector (at factor cost)

Service Sector	2000-01	2005-06	2006-07	2007-08	2008-09	2009-10	2010-11	2011-12	2012-13
Trade, hotels, & restaurants	14.6	16.7	17.1	17.1	16.9	16.5	17.2	18.0	25.1
	(5.2)	(12.2)	(11.1)	(10.1)	(5.7)	(7.9)	(11.5)	(6.2)	(5.2)
Trade	13.3	15.1	15.4	15.4	15.3	15.1	15.7	16.6	
	(5.0)	(11.6)	(10.8)	(9.8)	(6.7)	(8.5)	(11.5)	(6.5)	
Hotels & restaurants	1.3	1.6	1.7	1.7	1.5	1.4	1.5	1.5	
	(7.0)	(17.4)	(14.4)	(13.0)	(-3.3)	(1.9)	(10.8)	(2.8)	
Transport, storage, &	7.6	8.2	8.2	8.0	7.8	7.7	7.3	7.1	
communication	(9.2)	(11.8)	(12.6)	(12.5)	(10.8)	(14.8)	(13.8)	(8.4)	
Railways	1.1	0.9	0.9	1.0	0.9	0.9	0.8	0.7	
	(4.1)	(7.5)	(11.1)	(9.8)	(7.7)	(8.8)	(5.9)	(7.5)	
Transport by other means	5.0	5.7	5.7	5.6	5.5	5.3	5.3	5.4	
	(7.7)	(9.3)	(9.0)	(8.7)	(5.3)	(7.3)	(8.2)	(8.6)	
Storage	0.1	0.1	0.1	0.1	0.1	0.1	0.1	0.1	
	(6.1)	(4.7)	(10.9)	(3.4)	(14.1)	(19.3)	(2.2)	(9.4)	
Communication	1.5	1.6	1.5	1.4	1.4	1.4	1.1	0.9	
	(25.0)	(23.5)	(24.3)	(24.1)	(25.1)	(31.5)	(25.4)	(8.3)	
Financing, insurance, real estate,	13.8	14.5	14.8	15.1	15.9	15.8	16.0	16.6	**17.2**
& business services	(4.5)	(12.6)	(14.0)	(12.0)	(12.0)	(9.7)	(10.1)	(11.7)	**(8.6)**
Banking & Insurance	**5.4**	**5.4**	**5.5**	**5.5**	**5.6**	**5.4**	**5.6**	**5.7**	
	(-2.4)	**(15.8)**	**(20.6)**	**(16.7)**	**(14.0)**	**(11.4)**	**(14.9)**	**(13.2)**	
Real estate, ownership of ,	8.7	9.1	9.3	9.6	10.3	10.4	10.4	10.8	

dwellings & business services	(7.5)	(10.6)	(9.5)	(8.4)	(10.4)	(8.3)	(6.0)	(10.3)	
Community, social, & personal services	14.8	13.5	12.8	12.5	13.3	14.5	14.0	14.0	14.3
	(4.6)	(7.1)	(2.8)	(6.9)	(12.5)	(11.7)	(4.3)	(6.0)	(6.8)
Public administration & defence	6.6	5.6	5.2	5.1	5.8	6.6	6.1	6.1	
	(1.9)	(4.3)	(1.9)	(7.6)	(19.8)	(17.6)	(0.0)	(5.4)	
Other services	8.2	7.9	7.6	7.4	7.5	7.8	7.9	7.9	
	(7.0)	(9.1)	(3.5)	(6.3)	(7.4)	(7.2)	(8.0)	(6.5)	
Construction	6.0	7.9	8.2	8.5	8.5	8.2	8.2	8.2	8.2
	(6.1)	(12.8)	(10.3)	(10.8)	(5.3)	(6.7)	(10.2)	(5.6)	(5.9)
Total Services	50.8	53.1	52.9	52.7	53.9	54.5	54.4	55.7	56.5
	(5.4)	(10.9)	(10.1)	(10.3)	(10.0)	(10.5)	(9.8)	(8.2)	(6.6)
Total Services (incl. Construction)	56.8	61.0	61.0	61.2	62.4	62.7	62.6	63.9	64.8
	(5.5)	(11.1)	(10.1)	(10.3)	(9.4)	(10.0)	(9.8)	(7.9)	(6.5)
Total GDP	100.0	100.0	100.0	100.0	100.0	100.0	100.0	100.0	100.0
	(4.3)	(9.5)	(9.6)	(9.3)	(6.7)	(8.6)	(9.3)	(6.2)	(5.0)

Source: Economic Survey (2012-13)

Appendix 9.2

Registered insurers in India

Category	Public Sector	Private Sector	Total
Life Insurance	1	23	24
General Insurance	6	21	27
Reinsurance	1	0	1
Total	8	44	52

Source: IRDA

Appendix 9.3

Services Attracting Highest FDI Equity Inflows

S.NO.	Sector	2009-10	2010-11	2011-12 (Apr-Dec)	Capital Inflows (Apr 2000-Dec 2011)	% to Total (in USD)
1	**Services sector (financial & non-financial)**	19945 (4176)	15053 (3296)	21431 (4575)	142539 (31710)	20.1
2	**Telecommunications (radio paging, cellular mobile, basic telephone services)**	12270 (2539)	7542 (1665)	8969 (1989)	57035 (12544)	7.9
3	**Computer software & hardware**	4127 (872)	3551 (780)	2626 (564)	48940 (10973)	6.9
4	**Housing & real estate**	14027 (2935)	5600 (1227)	2544 (551)	48819 (10933)	6.9
5	**Construction activities (including roads & highways)**	13469 (2852)	4979 (1103)	7635 (1602)	46216 (10239)	6.5

Source: Economic Survey (2010-12)

Appendix 9.4

Insurance Penetration and Insurance Density in India

Year	Life		Non-Life		Industry	
	Density (USD)	Penetration (percentage)	Density (USD)	Penetration (percentage)	Density (USD)	Penetration (percentage)
1990	Na	1.41	Na	0.49	Na	1.90
1999	Na	1.39	Na	0.54	Na	1.93
2000	Na	1.77	Na	0.55	Na	2.32
2001	9.10	2.15	2.40	0.56	11.50	2.71
2002	11.70	2.59	3.00	0.67	14.70	3.26
2003	12.90	2.26	3.50	0.62	16.40	2.88
2004	15.70	2.53	4.00	0.64	19.70	3.17
2005	18.30	2.53	4.40	0.61	22.70	3.14
2006	33.20	4.10	5.20	0.60	38.40	4.80
2007	40.40	4.00	6.20	0.60	46.60	4.70
2008	41.20	4.00	6.20	0.60	47.40	4.60
2009	47.70	4.60	6.70	0.60	54.30	5.20
2010	55.70	4.40	8.70	0.71	64.40	5.10
2011	49.00	3.40	10.00	0.70	59.00	4.10

Source: Swiss Re, Various Issues

Appendix 9.5

Gross Domestic Product and Insurance Penetration

Year	GDP per capita at market price (in Rs.)	Penetration (in per cent)
1990	6987.03	1.90
1999	20211.09	1.93
2000	21368.14	2.32
2001	22652.36	2.71
2002	24018.25	3.26
2003	26506.56	2.88
2004	29772.35	3.17
2005	33393.93	3.14
2006	38277.24	4.80
2007	43823.29	4.70
2008	48787.37	4.60
2009	55366.04	5.20
2010	65727.77	5.10
2011	74666.78	4.10

Source: RBI Swiss Re, Various Issues

Appendix 9.6

Categorization of Indian states on the basis of average per capita NSDP

Category	States
Low-Income States	Bihar, Uttar Pradesh, Manipur, Assam, Madhya Pradesh, Jharkhand, Orissa, Jammu and Kashmir, Chhattisgarh, Rajasthan, Tripura, West Bengal, Mizoram, Meghalaya, Nagaland, Arunachal Pradesh
Middle-Income States	Andhra Pradesh, Karnataka, Himachal Pradesh, Uttarakhand, Kerala, Punjab, Tamil Nadu, Gujarat, Maharashtra, Andaman and Nicobar
High-Income States	Haryana, Puducherry, Sikkim, Chandigarh, Delhi, Goa

Source: Authors' calculation

Appendix 9.7

Average Per Capita NSDP[1] (in Rs.) and Insurance Penetration (in per cent) in Indian States

Category	2006-07		2007-08		2008-09		2009-10		2010-11		2011-12	
	p. c NSDP	Penetration	p. c NSDP	Penetration	p. c NSDP	Penetration	p. c NSDP	Penetration	p. c NSDP	Penetration	p. c NSDP	Penetration
Low-income states average	24081	1.31	27133	1.41	31045	1.10	34741	1.21	40273	1.04	45492	0.76
Middle-income states average	41621	1.83	48062	2.04	54397	1.41	62280	1.48	72455	1.21	81293	0.85
High-income states average	70976	2.54	79083	2.56	91650	1.99	110724	1.65	124863	1.48	136731	0.88

Source: Authors' calculation

[1] RBI, http://rbidocs.rbi.org.in/rdocs/Publications/PDFs/008T_BST130913.pdf.

LIST OF ABBREVIATIONS

AAI	Airport Authority of India
ADF	Airport Development Fee
AE	Advanced Estimates
AERA	Airports Economic Regulatory Authority of India
AFAS	ASEAN Framework Agreement on Services
AIT	Agreement of Information Technology
APEC	Asia Pacific Economic Cooperation
APMC	Agriculture Produce Market Committee
ARDL	Auto Regressive Distributed Lag Model
ASEAN	Association of Southeast Asian Nations
ATF	Aviation Turbine Fuel
ATM	Automated Teller Machine
BASA	Bilateral Air Service Agreements
BISAG	Bhaskaracharaya Institute for Space Application and Geo-informatics
BoP	Balance of Payments
BPL	Below Poverty Line
BPO	Business Process Outsourcing
CA	California
CAB	Current Account Balance
CAD	Current Account Deficit
CAGR	Compound Annual Growth Rate
CARICOM	Caribbean Community
CFO	Chief Financial Officer
CII	Confederation of Indian Industry
CSO	Central Statistical Organisation
CST Act	Central Sales Tax Act, 1956
CVD	Countervailing duty
DC	Debt Collection
DIAL	Delhi International Airport Limited
DIPP	Department of Industrial Policy and Promotion
DTH	Direct to Home
EAC	East African Community

ECB	External Commercial Borrowings
ECT	Error Correction Term
ER&D	Engineering & R&D Services
EU	European Union
FAO	Food and Agriculture Organization
FCC	Full Service Carrier
FDI	Foreign Direct Investment
FI	Foreign Investment
FICCI	Federation of Indian Chambers of Commerce and Industry
FII	Foreign Institutional Investor
FIPB	Foreign Investment Promotion Board
FTA	Free Trade Agreement
FY	Financial Year
GATS	General Agreement on Trade in Services
GCC	Gulf Cooperation Council
GCFR	Gross Capital Formation Rate
GDP	Gross Domestic Product
GDS	Gross Domestic Saving
GESIA	Gujarat Electronics & Software Industries Association
GFCE	Government Final Consumption Expenditure
GGDP	Growth rate of Gross Domestic Product
GIC	General Insurance Corporation
GIFT	Gujarat International Finance Tech
GNIE	Government not included Elsewhere
GNP	Gross National Product
GoI	Government of India
GSWAN	Gujarat State Wide Area Network
HP	Hodrick and Prescott
IATA	International Air Transport Association
IBEF	India Brand Equity Foundation
ICCPR	International Covenant on Civil and Political Rights
ICDR	Issue of Capital and Disclosure Requirements
ICT	Intra Corporate Transferees
IMF	International Monetary Fund
INR	Indian National Rupee
IRDA	Insurance Regulatory and Development Authority
IT	Information Technology

ITeS	Information Technology enabled Services
ITPL	International Tech Park
IWDMS	Integrated Workflow and Document Management System
KPO	Knowledge Process Outsourcing
LCC	Low Cost Carrier
LIC	Life Insurance Corporation
LM	Lee and Strazicich
MBA	Masters of Business Administration
MES	Modular Employable Skills
MFN	Most Favoured Nation
MIAL	Mumbai International Airport Limited
MNC	Multi-National Companies
MP	Member of Parliament
MRO	Maintenance, Repairs and Operations
NAFTA	North America Free Trade Agreement
NCAER	National Council of Applied Economic Research
NDP	Net Domestic Product
NFI	Net Factor Income
NIA	National Income Accounting
NNDI	Net National Disposable Income
NRG	Non Resident Gujarati
NSDP	Net State Domestic Product
NSSO	National Sample Survey Organisation
OECD	Organisation for Economic Co-operation and Development
OMC	Oil Marketing Company
PFCE	Private Final Consumption Expenditure
PIDDC	Product Infrastructure Development for Destination and Circuits
PN	Press Note
PP	Phillips-Perron
PPP	Public Private Partnership
PTA	Preferential Trade Agreement
QC	Quality Control
RBI	Reserve Bank of India
REER	Real Effective Exchange Rate
RTAs	Regional Trade Agreements
SADC	Southern African Development Community

SAST	Substantial Acquisition of Shares and Takeover Regulations
SC	Scheduled Caste
SDIS	Skill Development Initiative Scheme
SEZ	Special Economic Zones
SICN	Sachivalya Integrated Communication Network
SM	Services Import
ST	Scheduled Tribes
STPI	Software Technology Park of India
SWAGAT	State Wide Attention on Grievances through Application of Technology
SX	Services Export
UDF	User Development Fee
UK	United Kingdom
UNCTAD	United Nations Conference on Trade and Development
USA	United States of America
USD	United States Dollar
UTs	Union Territories
VAT	Value Added Tax
VECM	Vector Error Correction Model
WTO	World Trade Organization

CONTRIBUTORS

Aditi Sawant is working as Head of the Department of Economics, St. Xavier's College (Autonomous), Mumbai.

Hastimal G. Sagara is working as a Professor at the GLS Institute of Commerce, Ahmedabad.

Mini P. Thomas is pursuing a PhD under the UGC-Senior Research Fellowship Scheme at the Institute for Social and Economic Change, Bangalore.

Neha Shivani is pursuing a PhD (Economics) from the Central University of Gujarat, Gandhinagar.

Pralok Gupta is working as Consultant and Assistant Professor (Services and Investment) at the Centre for WTO Studies, Indian Institute of Foreign Trade, New Delhi. He has a PhD in Economics and Social Sciences from Indian Institute of Management (IIM) Bangalore.

Priyanka Gupta is working as a Research Analyst at AT Kearney, Gurgaon.

Ruchi Bhandari is working as an Assistant Professor at National Law University, Jodhpur.

Sazzad Parwez is pursuing a PhD (Economics) from the Central University of Gujarat, Gandhinagar.

Surabhi Singh is a doctoral student in International Organization at the Centre for International Politics, Organization and Disarmament, Jawaharlal Nehru University, New Delhi.

Vani Aggarwal is working as an Economic Analyst at TAC Economics, New Delhi.

Vidya C. T. is working as Assistant Professor at the Centre for Economic and Social Studies (CESS), Hyderabad. She received her PhD from the Indian Institute of Technology (IIT) Madras.